Still Crazy After All These Years

Newspaper Columns from a Sassy Southern Storyteller

By

Lee St. John

Lee St. John

D1527044

Acknowledgments

Erma Bombeck and Lewis Grizzard

Thank you for being you.

About Lee St. John

A #1 Amazon Bestselling author, humorist, 2019 Georgia Author of the Year Final Four in Essays, and known for her Southern Charm, Lee St. John writes observational comedy as she confesses and shares her wit in, *SHE'S A KEEPER! - Cockamamie Memoirs from a Hot Southern Mess* by Bienvenue Press. *No one* is safe - and she knows a lot of people - like Presidents of the United States, Professional Golf Champions, National Football League Super Bowl Champs, and even tales about the Mafia. Oh, and family and friends (even herself!)

TEACHER TATTLES and Other Southern Shenanigans is her second rascally memoir. The Tattles from the classroom are true stories. The Shenanigans? Might as well be.

She is featured in several anthologies including *CHICKEN SOUP FOR THE SOUL: Believe in Miracles*, Bienvenue Press' *Finally Home* (proceeds go to pet rescue organizations), and she was named an Erma Bombeck Humor Writer. Lee also is a popular and engaging guest speaker in the Southeast. She is found on every dang social media outlet.

Born, bred, and still living in Georgia, this retired teacher has been married for 38 years to her Southern gentleman. They have two adult sons, Lee and John, and she is a saint for raising them. They adore their tater-tot-shaped Schnauzer, OBie and Lee *loves* to laugh.

Lee St. John

2019 #1 Amazon Best Selling Author
2019 Georgia Author of the Year - Essays - Final Four
2020 Erma Bombeck Humor Writer
2020 Chicken Soup for the Soul Contributor

CONNECT WITH ME!

Facebook: https://www.facebook.com/leestjohnauthor
Instagram: https://instagram.com/leestjohnauthor/
Website and Blog: http://www.leestjohnauthor.com/
TV: Guest panel Atlanta and Company, Real Talk. WXIA-TV
Twitter: @LeeStJohnauthor
Newspaper: columnist Fayette-News (Fayetteville, Ga.)
Newspaper: former columnist for The Rockdale Citizen and The Newnan
Times-Herald
https://www.goodreads.com/author/show/14343509.Lee_St_John/blog
Pinterest: LeeStJohnAuthor
Pinterest: voice for OB the talking dog. Over 175K views
Peachtree City Library: voice for OB, the Storytelling Dog
Guest Speaker: popular Southern humorist of observational humor
Erma Bombeck Writer
National Society of Newspaper Columnists
Georgia Writers Association
Humorous Writers of America
Panel Member of Southern Living Magazine's THE FRONT PORCH
Can be found on Amazon.com

Table of Contents

I've Got a Secret

I've got a secret. My secret will be revealed before Valentine's Day 2020. I am not supposed to tell anyone until I am given the OK to do so. The people who have told me to keep quiet about the announcement understand I am dying to proclaim this news but when they contacted me, they mentioned, "We love the enthusiasm you will bring about the announcement, but please try your very hardest not to until…"

Will my secret play out like the *I've Got A Secret* game show which premiered on television June 19, 1952 and ran on CBS until April 3, 1967 even switching from black and white to color? This show was a derivative of the *What's My Line?* television show but instead of celebrity panelists trying to determine a contestant's occupation, the panel on *I've Got A Secret* tried to determine a contestant's "secret". Like this show, will it be something unusual, amazing, embarrassing, or humorous about me like it was for their participants? Will my secret be similar?

My instructions read, "You will receive another e-mail in a few weeks with more information…" Could the directive be like the American spy-fiction series, *The Man from U.N.C.L.E.*? This NBC broadcast followed secret agents who worked for a very secret international counterespionage and law-enforcement agency called U.N.C.L.E. Premiering on September 22, 1964 and completing its run, on January 15, 1968, it led the spy-fiction craze on television and by 1966 there were nearly a dozen imitators. Will I, too, be called into some secretive service?

My preparations continued, "…Our role…is to create a…plan that best suits you and allows you as much or as little involvement as you *choose*." Did this mean if I *choose* to accept my role like in *Mission: Impossible*? In 1966, this television series chronicled the exploits of a team of secret government agents known as IMF or Impossible Missions Force. Each episode opened with a fast-paced montage of shots from that episode which unfolded as the series' theme music played. Maybe I will receive my next directive from a voice delivered on a recording which then destroys itself. I do hope if by email, my computer does not blow up.

What if my instructions are like *I Spy*? I mean my email did read, "In order for us to provide you with the best possible support…please provide us with as much information…as you can…We are excited to be working with you…" *I Spy* was a secret-agent adventure television series that ran on NBC from September 1965 to April 15, 1968 and teamed two United States intelligence agents traveling undercover as international amateur and professional tennis players. In their reality, they just play against wealthy opponents in return for food and lodging. Their work involved chasing villains, spies, and beautiful women. I can't play tennis well, but I have been a golf groupie, if that helps, and know my way around golf courses.

My e-mail continued, "Be on the lookout for another e-mail in the next few weeks." Will it be similar to *Charlie's Angels*, an American crime drama TV series that aired on ABC from September 22, 1976 to June 24, 1981? With three female leads, it followed the adventures of these women working in a private detective agency in Los Angeles. Their unseen boss sent them crime-fighting operations assignments by speakerphone. At least he didn't have anything to self-destruct in five seconds like in *Mission: Impossible*.

Maybe my assignment will be more like *Get Smart*. Comedy is really more like me. This NBC series premiered on September 18, 1965 with the bumbling Don Adams character as Agent 86 parodying secret agent characters popular at that time.

This secret will be revealed soon enough, and I promise I will announce it here. Be on the lookout. You'll know what, when, where, why, and how. You already know WHO. Until then…hoping my computer doesn't self-destruct…

A Rose by Any Other Name Would Smell as Sweet

Remember the game show, I'VE GOT A SECRET, which began in 1952? Celebrity panelists tried to determine a contestant's occupation by asking questions of the participant who could only respond with "yes" or "no" answers. This secret occupation could be something unusual, embarrassing or humorous.

Well, I've got a secret, too. I wrote about an earlier secret I was carrying last year when I was told not to announce my addition to the CHICKEN SOUP FOR THE SOUL: Believe in Miracles anthology until several months later. The publishers, Simon & Schuster, wanted to keep the news quiet just a bit longer.

My secret today is about my name I use as an author, Lee St. John. If you have heard me speak at one of your meetings, you know that. But if you haven't invited me to come be a guest at one of your past meetings, you don't know that. I will tell you today why it is I have a nom de plume, a pseudonym, or pen name.

But first, why shouldn't I have a pen name? Samuel Clemons did. Benjamin Franklin used one. I'll even go so far to say William Shakespeare did, too.

Here is a list of a few others. Can you match the author with their pseudonym?

1. J.K. Rowling
2. Stephen King
3. Anne Rice
4. Nora Roberts

a. Ayn Rand
b. Ann Landers
c. Robert Galbraith
d. Dr. Suess

5.	Charles Dickens	e. Richard Bachman
6.	Louisa May Alcott	f. Curren Bell
7.	Charlotte Bronte	g. A. M. Barnard
8.	Emily Bronte	h. Boz
9.	Anne Bronte	i. Ellis Bell
10.	Ruth Crowley	j. Acton Bell
11.	Charles Lutwidge Dodgson	k. Lewis Carroll
12.	Eric Arthur Blair	l. George Orwell
13.	Mary Anne Evans	m. George Eliot
14.	Theodor Seuss Geisel	n. Anne Rampling
15.	Alisa Zinov'yevna Rosenbaum	o. J. D. Robb

In my case I thought my pen name sounded more like an author's name than my real one. But also, I was trying to get even with my own children. You see, I have two millennial sons who have never married, do not have children, and are not listening to anything I have to say. While writing my first book, I'd want to share one of my family stories with them about their childhood, but they didn't want to hear it. I'd ask "Why?" and they would answer that they lived it so why would they want to hear it again?

So, I did the next best thing to get their attention. I slapped their names on the cover. You've heard the saying, "Don't get mad. Get even." My oldest is Lee. My youngest is John. And I am a SAINT for having raised them.

Here are the pen names with the real ones.

Samuel Clemons – Mark Twain
Benjamin Franklin – Mrs. Silence Dogood

1. J.K. Rowling – Robert Galbraith
2. Stephen King – Richard Bachman

3. Anne Rice – Anne Rampling
4. Nora Roberts – J.D. Robb
5. Charles Dicksons – Boz
6. Louisa May Alcott – A.M. Barnard
7. Charlotte Bronte – Curren Bell
8. Emily Bronte – Ellis Bell
9. Anne Bronte – Acton Bell
10. Ruth Crowley – Ann Landers
11. Charles Lutwidge Dodgson – Lewis Carroll
12. Mary Anne Evans – George Eliot
13. Theodor Seuss Geisel – Dr. Seuss
14. Alisa Zinov'yevna Rosenbaum – Ayn Rand

And Lee St. John? – Gonna keep you guessing.

A Senior Moment

Dear Windsor, Cornwall, and Cambridge HRH families,

I have applied on your website for the position of *Senior Royal* now that the Duke of Sussex and his wife have decided to step down from their official duties to the crown. I became a *Senior* when I turned 65, therefore, I have one year experience, although some days I feel like I have more experience than others.

Even though I live "across the pond", I am one of the best Anglophiles. Here are my credentials:

1. I know my English royal history well. I know who did what to whom and when, where, and why it happened, especially during your family's Tudor reign. I live in a Tudor Revival home, therefore surrounded with reminders every day of the Tudor architecture and influences.

2. My Ancestry.com profile has placed my relations very close to royal blood since the 1600s. When I say close, my people probably hung around with yours as their minions.

3. I am a card-carrying Oxfordian. There are people in your country that probably don't know what that is, yet, here I am, an American and I am familiar with it. I mention this because I read that the Prince of Wales sympathizes with this theory ~~as I am hoping for some brownie points~~ of the authorship of Shakespeare. Perhaps having this same opinion with the Prince of Wales might provide favor toward this vacancy.

15

4. I've subscribed to "Majesty Magazine" for well over twenty years and have saved every issue because I am a ~~pack rat~~ collector. Because of this if there is something I am supposed to know but don't remember reading (doubtful), I can refer to my back issues.

5. My mother, a history teacher, told this story many times: when she was due to give birth to me, Queen Elizabeth II's coronation was to be televised. She worried she might miss coronation day. She was able to see it. I came along five days later. Therefore, I feel I have a special relationship with the Queen since our families had celebrations in June, 1953.

6. My middle name is Elizabeth.

7. My father's given name is Royal. Foreshadowing?

8. I awoke in the early morning of July 29, 1981 to see Prince Charles and Lady Diana's wedding ceremony live on television. Mother and I were in London when Prince William was born on June 21, 1982 and again I awoke early for William and Catherine's wedding. I'm respectful by writing Catherine and not Kate, even spelling it correctly.

9. When William's wedding to Catherine Middleton on April 29, 2011 at Westminster Abbey was a topic many were interested in, I decided to have a little fun with this. A month before the wedding, I wrote on my Facebook page that I was "invited to the ceremony. My invitation and ticket to enter the cathedral came in the mail today." As Royals, y'all know this wasn't ludicrous because William and Catherine *did* extend a few invitations to commoners

for their upcoming nuptials. As a young couple wishing to modernize the monarchy by having all kinds of people represented at their wedding, who better to invite than this Anglophile-know-it-all? It was ~~un~~believable.

Having been to Westminster Abbey, I remembered the layout. I wrote on Facebook that my ticket said I would be sitting in alcove "E", row 17, and seat number 32. I remarked that I was "totally surprised to be one of the 'regular/commoner' guests who applied to be invited to the wedding."

My friends knew how gaga I was over all y'all but still most knew it was a hoax. One social media friend was fooled. Excited, she wrote profusely on Facebook to make sure I memorized every detail of the wedding so that I could relay it to her when I came home.

See? I even have that impish streak, should you miss that comic relief in your family without Harry. Unlike Harry, I have respect for long lasting institutions and also as a *Senior* I have begun not to care what other people think.

I'd be honored if y'all chose me to be the newest *Senior* royal. I know how to curtsy correctly but not sure I can give up saying "y'all".

Soon to be royally yours, I hope,
Lee St. John

The Age of Innocence

There was no known drinking age before Prohibition in 1919. However, the drinking age was changed to twenty-one *after* Prohibition. Later the drinking age was lowered to eighteen in 1972 with the passage of the 26th Amendment partly because in the past it was widely debated as to which age the brain may have been considered fully developed. Many believed it happened in the mid to late teens. Then along came some evidence to suggest that development may happen around twenty. These days a consensus of neuroscientists agree that brain development likely persists until at least the mid-20s – possibly until the 30s. It is still widely debated as to which age the brain is considered "fully mature".

Which brings me to two stories forty years apart.

The first being with our newly hired twenty-six-year-old gardener. I say 'newly hired', because he is new to us. He is a college graduate in sound engineering and is looking for a job in his field…with this bad economy. So, we asked him in to manage some chores which involved a lot of bending over that hubby and I were not able to do without some help from our "nerve medicine" – the kind that upset those prohibiting this elixir during Prohibition.

This young man is multi-talented. So much so, we left him on his own to plant a few hostas in our garden. I placed the hosta, still in their containers, in the locations that I wanted him to dig a hole to plant them. Surveying his work, every hosta was in his correct place and nearly covered up with more potting soil. With rain coming our way on the radar, I told myself that if it didn't hit our area by five o'clock as anticipated, I would give the plants a good watering. Five o'clock came and went with no rain. As I started watering, I noticed something I wasn't used to. The hosta were planted in the exact location, but were planted still within their plastic containers! This mid-20s supposedly fully developed brain hadn't thought through the fact that roots needed room to grow. But he had never worked in horticulture either.

At the age of 22 in 1975, I had my first apartment in Atlanta. Oh, sure, I had lived in an apartment on campus with three other girls who shared all the household chores, but now I was living in Hot'Lanta with one other gal. Gone were the days of messy college-decor rooms. My new roommate and I were "practicing" on becoming adults like deep cleaning, mature decorating, and cooking gourmet meals.

One of my first adult-decisions was to host a dinner party. I was going to have friends over for a complete meal cooked only by me. I decided on asparagus (from the can), Pepperidge farm rolls (butter and heat), wedge iceberg salad (just cut off a wedge) with croutons (from the bag), cherry tomatoes, baby carrots (no chopping for either necessary), and started marinating the chicken the night before for extra flavor. I read carefully the directions from my family cookbook about how long to marinate the chicken, which I did.

But I left it on the counter!

The directions never said to place it back into the refrigerator to finish marinating. How was I supposed to know that? I was a novice cook, just like our novice gardener. No one had told me any differently. So, of course, the chicken was thrown away after I called my mother and she told me to do so. Although teary, I do not remember how I solved my chicken problem. Maybe KFC?

Anyhow, I see our gardener's dilemma. He didn't think it through – just like another twenty-something that didn't know about cooking any better either. During my trauma finding chicken to use for dinner, I probably could have used a sip of my "nerve medicine"!

Dear Class of 2020

Dear Class of 2020,

Congratulations to all high school graduates! Fifty years ago, I, too, was a Senior in high school, although not graduating until 1971. Nonetheless, in 1970, I was in my last academic year of high school. Now that I have the perspective of fifty years and especially as a retired educator, please let me take a moment to offer a few thoughts.

Even under these extreme circumstances, I know you all are proud to receive your diplomas. You have not left school behind, really, because you are now entering "Life School." You are about to enter the largest school of all. And I am not speaking of Georgia's oldest institutions of higher learning, the University of Georgia (38,920 enrollment), Georgia State University (53,000+ enrollment), Georgia Tech (36,489 enrollment), or one of the youngest and yet third largest school in the state, Kennesaw State University (almost 38,000 enrollment). You are entering the school of life. Instead of classrooms, you'll have offices, factories, and other professions. Instead of teachers, faculty, and administrators, you'll have superiors, supervisors, business, and religious leaders of the community. Exams and grades will not be held at regular schedules like what you are accustomed to, but there will be exams and your "grades" will be posted for everyone to see.

You will find all of school in life. It will take doing your homework to be successful. You'll find surprise quizzes when sudden problems arise and require mature judgment. The school spirit you once had for your hometown school will now be for America itself. The extracurricular activities which you enjoyed so much will now be based around your future families and social get-togethers.

Our school board cannot provide you with a routine graduation ceremony during this pandemic. You are the Seniors born the year of the September 11, 2001 terror attacks – the morning when there were four coordinated attacks by the Islamic terrorist group al-Qaeda against the United States. Those of us who remember 9/11 had our world changed forever as your world was just beginning. Now this virus has affected us, and you, again. You can still be genuinely proud of your accomplishments and know with all your reserve, the commodity not needed for immediate use but available if required, will go with you for any future contest, conflict, or dispute. Your graduating class is made of strong stuff.

Don't forget that the next "school bell" that rings will find you "in class" for the "required course" in ADULTHOOD, where the tests you are given will determine your future forever! So be glad that you've passed high school but remember not to flunk your future.

With Regards,
Lee St. John #1 Amazon Humor Writer

Math Word Problems

When both my boys were in pre-school, they were given a good foundation for future academics. I remember our three-year-old church pre-school introducing age-appropriate math and other curriculum. At the end of the year, the average three year was to collect and count out loud with three teddy bear shaped pieces. What the teacher was expecting was each child would see several bears on the table and collect them one by one and hand them to the teacher while counting as they did so. "One bear. Two, Three." They were counting their own age.

When it was my eldest's turn at this instruction to see if he was capable of showing what three meant, he collected three at one time and handed them over to his teacher. When it was my baby's turn, eight years later, he grabbed five and subtracted two. Our pre-school teacher, having taught both of my boys, told me that she always thought our first child was smart with his adding the bears before giving her the answer, but when the youngest had his turn she was astonished that at three he was *subtracting*.

It was then I knew their aptitude for math should make it easy for them. Our eldest did well throughout his years in school. Our youngest performed the same *until* the NEW MATH was introduced in his 9th grade year. That year, the Common Core standards offered a new approach to math that emphasized more conceptual forms of understanding and "…if states and districts implemented the reform well, the instruction will give students deeper math skills. Common Core math also has the potential to better prepare students for a career."

I get this lofty idea. But the state didn't start this new math just in elementary school but as soon as possible, which meant, those who had learned one way of deciphering math problems were jerked into something totally new, without preparation, to begin how to understand math. My youngest was in 9th grade and it was one of the worst times of his life. Not only him, but about 75% had to take even another math class at the same time to repair and supplement whatever they were behind on with the new regular, but foreign, math class. It was like being thrown into the deep end with hopes you will just survive.

These supplemental classes also took away from a time slot for learning something else besides math. His father, an accountant, couldn't help. He was schooled in old math. I was just a math dummy. This is how word-problems in math looked to me:

1. If you purchase two of the books, *Math for Dummies*, each costing $16.99, when the clerk adds the total and it comes to $50.00, is he incorrect?

2. If the teacher says, "You have ten chocolate cakes and someone asks for two, how many do you have left?" And if the student answers, "Ten" and the teacher continues, "Okay, well what if somebody forcibly takes two of the cakes, how many would you have left?" and the student answers, "Ten AND a dead body", is the student incorrect?

3. Is this restaurant sign correct? "Today's special – Buy one Fish & Chips for the price of two and receive a second Fish & Chips *absolutely free*!"

4. If the teacher loudly comments, "Don't worry, I'm not actually saying anything important up here, in the

front of the room, about your lesson" what percentage of the class of students will answer with, "So, if I just do my homework, my grade will improve?"

5. On the first day of face-to-face instruction at school, students are required to bring 30 pencils, 64 crayons, 20 pens, 12 rulers, and 10 notebooks. How many of these items will be left after a month of instruction? Answer: ONE pencil found on the ground, or classroom, or hallway.

And it will probably be missing an eraser and no lead at the point.

Hope 2021 improves for teachers and parents!

Smarty Pants!

I remember one day in the 1990s my middle school principal mentioned in a faculty meeting about the reciprocity of Florida allowing one of our Georgia teachers to be able to teach there without having to jump through their state requirements to do so.

I had never used that word before. I knew it must have the root word reciprocal so why not just say reciprocal agreement? Show-off.

Let's look at that word. Here are some synonyms: cooperation, exchange, mutuality, **reciprocality**, reciprocation, partnership, relationship. I bet there are some synonyms in that group you would use on a daily basis and then there are some that are a little overbearing, uppity, high and mighty, cavalier, or audacious.

What is a word for someone with a large vocabulary? It's sesquipedalian. In reality, even the word sesquipedalian is in fact sesquipedalian. It can also be used to describe someone or something that overuses big words, like a philosophy professor or a chemistry textbook. Do you know any one like that?

Does knowing big words make you smart? Intelligent people tend to be more well-read. It's important to note that a large vocabulary is more than just knowing a few big words. ... The more you improve your vocabulary, the more your intelligence will increase.

Have you heard of the Bell Curve? This graph shows the spread of values of anything affected by the cumulative effects of randomness. Founded in the 19th century, there's no shortage of those: from stock market jitters to human heights and IQ. Many phenomena follow at least a rough approximation of the Bell Curve, with the most common value in the center, and rarer, more extreme values to either side. An intelligence quotient (IQ) is a total score derived from a set of standardized tests or subtests designed to assess human intelligence.

The curve peaks at the top with a score of an average 100. Sixty-eight percent of us fall in between the scores of 85 and 115. Ninety-six percent of us fall in between 70 and 130. You can see the pattern. The bottom of the bell graph has the fewest percentages of either IQ extreme. Special education classes in school for both slower and gifted students are designed for both ends of the graph curve.

The book, *The Bell Curve*, published 1994, states "Inequality of endowments, including intelligence, is a reality. Trying to pretend that inequality does not really exist has led to disaster. Trying to eradicate inequality with artificially manufactured outcomes has led to disaster. It is time for America once again to try living with inequality, as life is lived: understanding that each human being has strengths and weaknesses, qualities we admire and qualities we do not admire, competencies and incompetencies, assets and debits; that the success of each human life is not measured externally but internally; that all of the rewards we can confer on each other, the most precious is a place as a valued fellow citizen."

The following order will be my *guess* of using the reciprocity synonyms and ranking them to intelligence from low to high by how likely we use the chosen word:

1. Would you use the word <u>exchange</u> more likely when talking about doing something in return?
2. Or would you use <u>cooperation</u>?
3. <u>Partnership</u>?
4. How about <u>mutuality</u>?
5. I had never heard of <u>reciprocality</u> until today.

How would *you* have ranked these synonyms?

Want to try another? Do you use overbearing, high and mighty, uppity, cavalier, or audacious words? Or do you have hippopotomonstrosesquipedaliophobia - the fear of long words?

Personally, I think if you use reciprocality, as seen above, in your everyday conversation when discussing return agreements, you might be a:

1. Know-it-all
2. Big mouth
3. Bragger
4. Egomaniac
5. Braggadocio

Or in other words, a SHOWOFF!

Don't Know How Good They've Got It

I have been the keeper of the vintage and dear possessions both my parents and my husband's parents left behind. We have purged but there are just some things one can't part with. If only my children were as sentimental. I asked my oldest one day about why he wasn't more nostalgic? He gave a great answer. He said, "Mom, I grew up in a generation where everything was new and continued to be improved really fast...like computers."

He's right. He's a millennial and lives in, really, a throw-away generation. He's never known life without the internet and other fast advancements. Think about the new iPhones that young people (and us) get every few years. Yes, we (they) want it faster, better, and easier.

But here's just a few things my son and his younger brother have rarely, or never, experienced.

1. Mailing a letter. Years ago, maybe.
2. Using all their fingers to type. My mother encouraged me to take typing lessons and it helped me get every job to which I applied.
3. They never had to get up to change the channel. All they have ever known was a remote.
4. What about having only four channels? They never had to deal with that!

5. Remember the video game cartridges when you blew on them to get the dust out. Well, maybe they did that a few times.

6. Did they ever write notes in class? Play paper football or make a cootie catcher?

7. With the 'Whole Language' concept in education **which impaired learning how to** *spell*, something was lost in translation.

8. We didn't have this, but it could be they felt left out at their friends' homes when there was clapping to get the lights on or off.

9. Do they even understand what a dial rotary phone is and how it operates? Remember how frustrating it was to get the wrong number more than once and starting all over again?

10. Borrowing a quarter to make a phone call or make a collect call.

11. Need directions? All we had was to stop and ask a real human. (I still stop and ask sometimes.)

12. They don't have to wait for their favorite song to come on the radio so they can record it.

13. Well, I am happy for them, because they don't have to stand by to watch their favorite storyline by having to wait for all the commercials to end. That is a luxury.

14. Don't have to pull up cell phone antennas.

15. Never have they had to stay home to watch their TV show during the actual day and time it aired.

16. They were never bothered with manually rolling down a window or reach across the car seat to unlock a door for someone.

17. They didn't write in cursive for very long.
18. Carry a date or address book and buy refills for them. (That is still one my favorite old-school things to do!)
19. Put film in a camera (oh, and accidentally have the camera pop open only to render the whole roll blank).
20. Go to a Drive-in movie (and fight over who got to lie across the back ledge of the car).

I hope in time something will catch their fancy about their own life journey and put them in a mood to reminiscence. Then maybe they will know why their mama is a keeper of memories from my past and theirs.

*** My oldest son majored in IT with an MBA becoming Director, Learning and Production Environments at Georgia State University at the age of thirty-four. He lives in a fast-changing world. No wonder.

No Surprises Here

Why is anyone surprised that the Southeastern Football Conference is the fiercest in the land? How could one be surprised that they (we) are the most powerful conference in all of conferences if not only by our strength, stamina, and brute, but also because of the mascots chosen to represent us in the fight. It stands to reason that the SEC will dominate.

Our teams consist of Clawing Tigers, Biting Bulldogs, Red Elephant Stampedes, Scratching Wildcats, Man-eating Gators, Relentless Fighting Cocks, Determined Volunteer Military, Scary Razorbacks, an unbeatable 12th man player, a seafaring captain that defends his ship against pirates, and even though we once had a gentlemanly and mannerly colonel, today he is a towering Black Bear.

Who could lose a competition with these figureheads? The following mascots would not stand a chance. Let's consider the matchups. In alphabetical order, here are some examples:

Aristocat – the costumed mascot of the Tennessee State University Tigers and Lady Tigers. *How will she fight like a cat dressed in pearls, high heels, and her fur coat?*

The Battling Bishop – mascot of Ohio Wesleyan. *What is his strength? I think he'll be praying for it to end as he gets the 'you-know-what' beaten out of him.*

The Blue Devil- a costumed student who serves as mascot of Duke University. *Blue is a calm color. Ask the design experts. Fire red would be a better devil color choice. So, this Blue Devil is way out of his league. He should be teaming up with the Bishop and they might make a partial team.*

Boll Weevil – the mascot of the University of Arkansas – Monticello. *This mascot was named by the school president in 1925. It feeds on cotton buds and flowers (how sweet) and migrated into the United States from Mexico in the late 19th century. It had infested all U.S. cotton-growing areas by the 1920s. Since 1978, it has been eradicated. ERADICATED! There's a good word for SEC's football performances and that is exactly what would happen to those pesky bugs playing against the SEC.*

Cayenne – a costumed chili pepper for the Ragin' Cajuns of Louisiana-Lafayette. *A chili pepper? Oh, it might burn your tongue for a few moments but the rest of you ain't hurtin'.*

Charlie Cardinal – the cardinal mascot of Ball State University. *The northern Cardinal was named because of its brilliant plumage and it is a hardy bird that is capable of living in almost any kind of environment. It is also known for its beautiful song. This bird is pretty and talented. Yeah, that's scary. Should be in another kind of competition – like a beauty pageant?*

Chip – the costumed buffalo of the University of Colorado. *Now this could be a frightening animal – it has size and strength, but they give him a comical name – Chip. What's he going to do? Throw buffalo chips to distract the opposing players? Messy, but not life-threatening. At least they have a sense of humor.*

Colonel Ebirt – the former mascot of the College of William & Mary Tribe. *The name "Ebirt" is "Tribe" spelled backwards and is a green blob dressed in colonial garb.*

That colonial get-up, all stuffy and proper, would hold anybody back from playing at their best. Not to mention if they brought their muskets. Historically, it took an average of twenty seconds to load and fire a smoothbore (rubber bullets) black powder musket. A lot could happen in twenty seconds. You might step in unnoticed buffalo dung or get a left-over buffalo chip thrown at you.

<u>Cowboy Joe</u> – the live Shetland pony mascot of the University of Wyoming. *A short pony? That's telling. "We came to play with our team of ponies which are used mostly for children's enjoyment." Say, what?*

<u>Damien, The Great Dane</u> – the mascot of the University of Albany. *Besides probably getting knocked over, I can't imagine any more damage than that.*

<u>The Oregon Duck</u> – the mascot of the Oregon Ducks. *My mother used to say when something was unpleasant, "I'd rather be pecked by ducks." If you outrun them, surely that won't happen. Waddle, Waddle. And what's a peck anyway?*

<u>Dooley</u> – skeleton mascot for Emory University. *Hey! Emory! Break a leg or an arm. You will.*

<u>Dusty</u> – the Dust Devil mascot for Texas A&M International University. A dust devil is a strong, well-formed, and relatively short-lived whirlwind, ranging from small to large. *Even large and strong it's short-lived. Maybe some concern until half-time but only because you can't see who is running the ball with all that dust. Tasmanian Devil? Now <u>that</u> would worry me. Chomp, chomp.*

<u>Dutch</u> – the Flying Dutchman - a costumed mascot of Hope College. The Flying Dutchman is a legendary ghost ship that can never make port and is doomed to sail the

oceans forever. *Not worried one bit. It will never make it to the game.*

The Explorer – mascot of La Salle University. *Our Captain in the SEC has got this.*

The Fighting Okra – name of the unofficial mascot of Delta State University since 1980s. Featured in David Letterman's "Top Ten Worst Mascots List". *Do they think because they are slimy, they are going to slip through our defenses? Not a chance.*

Fighting Pickle – mascot of University of North Carolina School of the Arts. *Oh, I get it now…just put the word FIGHTING in front of whatever and you think that makes you ruff, tuff, stuff. They are the ones that will be in a pickle.*

The Friar – a costumed Dominican Friar of Providence College. *He's huddled on the field with last week's Ohio Wesleyan's Bishop trying to figure out a way to get the hell outta the contest.*

Gaylord – Campbell University's camel mascot - even-toed ungulate that bears distinctive fatty deposits known as "humps" on its back. Camels have been domesticated by humans for about 5000 years. They are used for riding and to carry things. *I know they couldn't use Cool Old Joe Camel, but wouldn't it be nifty if they did at least for image? Gaylord just ain't cuttin' it.*

Goldy the Gopher – mascot for University of Minnesota. *They are nothing but pests. Our mascots have already read the Gopher Bait Guide. They can easily be manipulated.*

Gompei – the bronzed head of a now deceased goat mascot at Worcester Polytechnic Institute. *A dead mascot. No threat.*

The Governor – mascot of Austin Peay University. *We all know how conniving politicians can be but go ahead, scheme away…the SEC will out-wit you.*

Grubby Grubstake – a miner mascot of South Dakota School of Mines and Technology. *The only thing scary about this mascot is his pick ax and since there are no weapons allowed on the field, they'll be kept in the dark about how tough we really are… without props.*

Gus the Goose – costumed mascot of the Washington College Shoreman. *I don't see how in the world a wobbly goose, or even a gaggle of them, are going to threaten any of our mascots. Most of ours will just call them 'lunch'.*

Herbie Husker – the costumed mascot of the University of Nebraska. *This mascot may come buttered, popped, salted, white, greasy, puffy or found in balls or singular kernels. No matter, this corn will be creamed!*

The Virginia Tech Hokies – the word "hokie" originated when a man wrote it into a cheer for a contest. And he won! He says he made it up as a way of getting attention, but its origins are traced back to 1842 and means "hooray." However, the "hokie mascot" is really a turkey. A turkey! The bird is a "HokieBird" which has evolved from a turkey. Virginia Tech teams were once called the "gobblers"! *OK. Just stop it. Giving you more description does not make this mascot any better. Writers providing this information just need to stop it now. I can find nothing redeeming about this mascot name. I mean, I could say that Benjamin Franklin once wanted the turkey to be the national bird instead of the eagle, but that doesn't help. Even that kind of information just makes it worse.*

Jack the South Dakota State University Jackrabbit mascot - Jackrabbits are not rabbits (despite their name). They belong to group of animals called hares and are often treated as pests because they quickly destroy crops and have a ferocious appetite. *So, they will eat the turf, get a full tummy, and then what? Probably a nap. Or be busy proliferating. Both would seem to take precedence over playing football.*

John Poet – the mascot of Whittier College. Both college and mascot are named for John Greenleaf Whittier. *Sensitive and heartfelt, John Poet would probably be happiest writing poetry along side the football fence than being in the trenches as he writes in his poem, In School-Days – "Still sits the school-house by the road…" Whatever…The SEC mascots should watch out. The only thing they should worry about is tripping over this unnoticed bundle of literary terms near the field.*

Keggy the Keg – this anthropomorphic beer keg is the unofficial mascot of Dartmouth College. Up until 1971, Dartmouth's mascot was an Indian. *Politically incorrect, I suspect. But a beer keg is a better choice? However, this is my personal favorite mascot. I don't think they are serving Gatorade to their players during the game. This would definitely help the opposing team. Hic-up!*

The Leprechaun – the mascot for Notre Dame. These little bearded men, wearing a coat and hat and who partake in mischief, are solitary creatures who spend their time making and mending shoes and have a hidden pot of gold at the end of the rainbow. If captured by a human, they often grant three wishes in exchange for their freedom. *Wish One to an SEC tackle, "You win." Wish Two: "Ok, you win big." Win Three: "One of your conference teams will go on to be*

#1 in the nation. Now, please let me go! I've got to go mend this hole in my shoe where your cleat stepped on it."

Mo the Mule – the official mascot of the University of Central Missouri. *Stubborn. You can lead a mule to the football field, but you can't make them play.*

Montezuma the Aztec Warrior - mascot of University of Central Missouri. *With all the symptoms of Montezuma's Revenge, they will never even make it on the field.*

Mortimer the Gopher – mascot of Goucher College. Seldom above ground and liking moist soil, they burrow then tunnel their way where the soil is softer and will visit vegetable gardens, lawns, or farms. *Any SEC canine mascot will have a 'field day' digging for them even if they are in a packed football field soil. Don't forget some fields have artificial turf, and if so, those boogers are doomed because they may run, but they will have no place to hide.*

MUcaw – the mascot of Mount Union, Alliance, Ohio. The macaw parrot squawks and screeches. They can be quite deafening and ear piercing. They are inclined to whistle or imitate sounds and noises they hear. *I would advise keeping this loud-colored and loud-voiced mascot away from the coaches as they shout plays from the side lines. A macaw will loudly repeat these play calls for all to hear which will eventually be deciphered by the SEC teams if used a lot. Also, don't forget the macaw whistles. How in the world are you going to keep them from imitating the refs? Think of the confusion these birds will cause. What kind of penalty will the referees decide to issue for these imitations? Good news for all SEC teams.*

Oakie – the costumed acorn mascot of SUNY-ESF. *I mean, really? Crunch.*

Ollie the Owl – mascot of Brandeis University. *His head will be spinning as he thinks, "Which way did they go?"*

Otto the Orange – mascot of Syracuse University. *No competition here. They will be 'freshly squeezed'.*

Pete and Penny – two emperor penguins dressed in scarfs and stocking caps for Youngstown State University. Besides posturing in their tuxedos and despite their large size, emperor penguins can dive to a depth of 1800 feet and stay submerged for up to eighteen minutes. *Oh, that's good to know while they visit the SEC's humid and ninety-degree temps during the games. Yeah, that talent should work for them. NOT!*

Can they even get more ridiculous? Oh, wait…they can…

Peter the Anteater – mascot for the University of California – Irvine since 1965. *This is where the SEC fans come into play. They throw out all their food wrapper remnants onto the field while the SEC teams wait for the ants to show up and then while the anteaters are gobbling up the ants, we pounce. How sneaky! How genius! Those West-Coast schools think we southerners are slow. Suck on that, UC!*

Petey the Penman - The brawny physique of the original Penmen, with its muscular legs, arms and torso, was designed to represent the rugged character of the original New England settlers, yet features the character holding a basketball in one hand and a quill in another. *This ain't no basketball game or literary meet. He's not even trying to hide his football inadequacy.*

Purple Cow – the gold-spotted mascot of Williams College, Massachusetts. No one seems to know how or why this cow with a yellow streak became the school's official mascot. *Yellow Streak? Think about it. We'll own them.*

Roady, the roadrunner (three of them) – a costumed mascot of California State University, Bakersfield, Metropolitan State University of Denver, and university of Texas, San Antonio. This great state bird of New Mexico (and yet not a mascot in sight in New Mexico) are good luck as well as symbols of strength. Their feathers have been used to ward off evil. Running up to fifteen miles per hour, they can sprint up to twenty-six mph. This is the fastest sped for any bird that can also fly. Created by Chuck Jones in 1948 for Warner Brothers, the most famous roadrunner is the Road Runner. *Although coyotes do catch and eat roadrunners, although Wile E. Coyote never did, wouldn't several SEC mascots be able to do the same? Except, with all that voo-doo stuff, who would want to? I think they have become my favorite SEC adversary. Who would want to tempt voo-doo? That's something beyond the playing field.*

The Stanford Tree – a dancing conifer of indeterminate species official mascot of Stanford Band and the unofficial mascot of Stanford University. *I wouldn't claim a dancing tree either. Imagine this "thing" on the football field. What kind of dance does a tree do, anyway? Swaying back and forth? I can't think of a dance name it could do and win a football game.*

Sycamore Sam – the happy forest animal costume of no particular species but looks like a blue fox or dog. Mascot of the Indiana State Sycamores. *No one knows what this animal is, but it just stays happy all the same. And why isn't it a tree instead of some non-descriptive happy animal? The real match up should be the Stanford Tree vs. The Sycamore Tree. Now that would be a sight. I bet you could guess how they got ahold of Dartmoth's Keggy the Keg juice since one just dances around and the other one is happy all the time. Something's not right about this.*

Terrible Swede – a costumed mascot of Bethany College in Kansas. *Oh, so instead of putting the word 'fighting' in front of this mascot name, they use 'terrible'. If I were a Swede, I'd be offended just like the Native Americans were opposed to using their name and image for the Washington Redskins. What would Erik the Red or Leif Erickson's ancestors say?*

Testudo – a costumed Diamondback Terrapin of the University of Maryland College Park. *Unless they send in their female team who tend to grow larger, the male terrapins don't stand a chance. Oh, and let me say, the females grow to about 7.5 inches to the male's 5.1-inch size. BIG difference.*

Thresher – the threshing stone mascot of Bethel College. *What is a threshing stone you ask? It's a roller-like tool used for threshing wheat and pulled by horses. Horses! It needs horses to move its immovable self around. What about having a stone-cold mascot? Ridiculous.*

Vixen – the mascot of Sweet Briar College. A female fox or a spiteful or quarrelsome woman. *Boy, what if a male had come up with this mascot name – I can hear it now – "Misogynist"! I can't see a bunch of women with these traits wanting to play football in the first place. They'd be arguing the ref's calls all the time. Well, that's how I see it. But I am just "Sexist". (Can a woman be sexist?)*

41

WebstUR – the spider mascot of the Richmond spiders. *Unless they are poisonous, I don't see their threat.*

Wilbur and Wilma Wildcat – the *married* costumed mascots of the University of Arizona. *They are so in love, they must be domesticated and therefore, non-threatening. Give them twenty years of marriage and then see if they are more hostile on the field.*

WuShock – an anthropomorphic shock of wheat. Mascot of Wichita State University. *Shocking!*

Back to the Future

On February 19, 2020, more than a dozen people set out on a twenty-five-day adventure rafting the Colorado River through the Grand Canyon. When they left, the Democratic debate in Las Vegas was to be held that evening with Bernie Sanders having a double-digit lead. In mainland China, cases of coronavirus were showing signs of decline.

Their enterprise came to an end on March 21 with a disturbing reality. As they paddled to shore for the last time, the first other human being they'd encountered in nearly a month asked this question, "Have you had any contact with the outside world?"

The group shrugged and said no. Then the man sighed and continued while rolling his eyes, "The world is going crazy. You've got a lot to hear. The stock market crashed, toilet paper is out everywhere, Italy closed its border, and the NBA isn't doing games anymore."

Imagine hearing all that after twenty-five days of being off the grid. I found some other headlines that these rafters also missed and might catch their interest. All are true but one. Can you guess which one is not real?

Planters made an announcement in late January on Twitter: Mr. Peanut died. You know the one…that cartoon peanut with a top hat and monocle. Mr. Peanut, according to the ad they released, sacrificed himself after a car crash to save his friends. The announcement was shocking but the reaction to it was more shocking *because* of the reactions to it: people *loved* that Mr. Peanut died. They hoped he roasted in hell. His death was celebrated all over the internet. There was cheering in the streets. Who would have thought people cared about Mr. Peanut that much. That would have a big shock coming back to reality with that news, too.

Here's another surprise for the group. People all over the world stepped up to donate to Australia's cause of dealing with devastating wildfires. Kaylen Ward, one enterprising woman, went above and beyond by sending nude photos to anyone who donated at least $10 to the organizations working to put out the fires. All she asked was to send proof that you donated. And guess what? She raised over $1 million, and she gave herself a new nickname: the "Naked Philanthropist".

Hey, Rafters – would you believe this? There have been mysterious sightings of swarms of drones in the sky over Colorado and Nebraska. Those reporting this development claim they are "as big as cars, flying in groups in grid patterns at night." Authorities expressed that there is nothing weird about the flying objects. Of course, conspiracy theories proliferated with some believing in aliens while others are convinced it's the military and they are not admitting to any of it. So, mysterious UFO sightings start this decade and while you were rafting, you failed to hear about it.

Brad Pitt and Jennifer Aniston met up backstage at the 2020 SAG awards where they were both winners in the respective categories and where the paparazzi went crazy trying to tie them back together after fifteen years apart. Rumors started flying as they were photographed together being rather cozy as many body language experts noticed. This will make great fodder for the remaining year.

And finally, how surprised will these adventurists be once they face reality and find their own toilet paper shortage. But never fear. If they are traumatized, all they have to do is call Stanley Morgan of Morgan & Morgan Attorney at Law to see if they may be entitled to compensation!

Beating the System

I turned sixty-six last week and last year gave myself the gift of Medicare. It's the gift that keeps on giving as I've used it quite a bit this past year and especially this past week. Long story but thank goodness it wasn't my writing hand, and I can still type.

I haven't had to jump through any cognitive hoops yet. But I have some much older friends who have. These women get together on Wednesdays for their weekly bridge group. It's a neighborhood group and was founded by one of the oldest members about twenty-five years ago.

It has become very close-knit because after all, meeting every week for twenty-five years for Kitchen Bridge, they tend to be able to chat and learn about each other in a casual setting rather than in Duplicate Bridge where no talking is allowed. Kitchen Table Bridge (sometimes called party bridge or rubber bridge) is one method of playing 'contract bridge' and allows the players to visit and talk with the players at your table.

Whereas Duplicate Bridge is highly competitive and once the bidding has begun, general conversation is not encouraged at the table. Bridge etiquette in duplicate allows you to exchange pleasantries with your partner and the opponents, but during play there should not be any discussion of the hands. One should wait until the game is over for the post-mortems.

A plus to the talkative bunch is that they are able to exchange information about their families, their health, their doctors, and such. Which is what happened recently. This bridge group of at least twenty ladies are all over the age of sixty-five except for a couple of gals. The Alzheimer's topic came up. Early detection of Alzheimer's is important and yet the Alzheimer's Foundation of America announce that general practitioners currently miss about fifty percent of dementia cases. So, there is now an annual free Medicare wellness exam that includes cognitive memory tests to help increase the rate of early diagnosis of dementia which is included in the wellness check-up.

Overheard recently at bridge -

"Oh, Millie, I so wish I didn't have to take that test when I visit my general practitioner for my yearly wellness exam. He asks me to read aloud from the list and then waits until the end of the exam to ask me to recite them again from memory. I become so nervous when I am supposed to recite the nouns, *in order*. I know I am forgetful in many areas, but these words have no relevance to me to help me remember. I mean, 'monkey, basketball, stool, doorknob, giraffe, and palm tree'?

"Eudora, you go to my doctor, too, right?" Millie asks.

"I go to him," interrupted Phyllis. "I have had that same test with those same words, too. I get being nervous, Millie. I shouldn't be but I feel like if I fail it will be recorded in my file, so I stay nervous the entire time and when I get nervous, I can't think!"

Eudora chimes in, "Ladies, looks like we *all* go to the same physician, so we need to devise a plan to conquer our fear of this test. Phyllis says she remembers it's the same words that Millie was tested on. What if our doctor is giving us all the same words? I believe he does!"

"I know," says Millie. "Whoever has the first appointment with him for next year should come back and tell us what the words are so the rest of us can be prepared and we will rotate who goes first each year so the rest of us can reciprocate the next time. Want to?"

And because they did, "The women started receiving 100% on their tests for the next several years."

And to think it all started with Kitchen Table Bridge. If it had been Duplicate Bridge, they never would have hatched this plan.

Traditionally Speaking

I subscribe to *Southern Living Magazine* and am a member of their board, THE FRONT PORCH. I have purchased this magazine my entire adult life. I never knew my mother not to have a subscription, either. I mostly duplicated mama's shopping habits, too, except to purchase Hellman's mayonnaise whereas she bought Kraft. Oh, and she washed her clothes in Tide but I use Arm and Hammer.

But I am getting off topic.

I do not think I was chosen because of my faithfulness to *Southern Living* but maybe it didn't hurt as they periodically ask my opinion about: proposed topics, advertising, and my advice on which direction the magazine should take for the future. I do not get free copies of the magazine for this service. I am just a representative from a certain age group, I guess. (They do reward their board members for answering their survey questions with $25 or $100 quarterly drawings.) They haven't picked my name although I have been on the board about five years.

This article appeared on-line and certainly brought back memories: "Southern Traditions We Want to Bring Back – And You Will Too!" There were twenty-three traditions. Let's see if we have continued any of these customs.

1. *Saying Please and Thank You*. This may not be just Southern speak but television anchor and a former Georgia Junior Miss from Dalton, Deborah Norville, wrote a book entitled, *Thank You Power: Making the Science of Gratitude Work for You. Please* investigate and *thank you* for your time if you do.

2. *Saying Sir or Ma'am.* This is definitely a Southern expression. My younger son, age twenty-seven, habitually does this. But some may take offense because they might connect it with being old. They shouldn't worry. Old is always fifteen years from now.

3. *Proper Table Manners.* I sent both my boys to Cotillion classes so that they didn't think they were the only ones having to practice table etiquette at home. They still remember the phone goes left of the entrée fork.

4. *Cursive Writing.* Oops. Second son's is such hen scratch. Does this mean that his destiny is to become a doctor?

5. *Hand Written Thank You Notes.* My boys have their own monogrammed note cards. I even considered what my children's name would be by how the initials looked in a monogram.

6. *Recipe Cards.* I lovingly have kept my mother's original recipe box with her handwritten recipes. Her chicken recipes are even better than the New York Times Bestseller, *Fifty Shades of Chicken* by FL Fowler, a parody which claims "Fifty chicken recipes, each more seductive than the last, in a book that makes every dinner a turn-on."

7. *Sunday Suppers.* My family is a small one but those with a large family, do you sometimes think, "Are these people really my relatives?"

8. *Holding the Door Open for Others.* I've done this and said either "Thank you" to other females or "What a gentleman" for the males who do this

kindness for me. But sometimes today you can't tell the difference. Guess I'll just have to say "thank you" to all. See #1.

9. *Welcoming New Neighbors.* Did you know that Amazon sells a Bathroom Guest Book? Under this title it says, "Please sign in while sitting down." It's only $12.80 with FREE one-day shipping and FREE returns. You save $5.18. Thought you would want to know. Wouldn't think this would make a neighborly good first impression gift, though.

10. *A Good Handshake.* In 2020, 2021 – what is a handshake?

11. *Phone Calls.* What are those? Think they mean text messages?

12. *Punctuality.* For dinner parties stick with "Five minutes early is on-time. On-time is late. Being late is unacceptable." I am bad about punctuality for cocktail parties, though, because I know what it feels like to have guests come too early. There are always hiccups before guests arrive. I will hide behind the old adage. "Better to arrive late than ugly."

13. *Dressing Up For Church.* It has been a long Southern tradition, especially for women, who frequently topped off their outfits with a church hat. Anybody out there still wearing their Sunday Best? (This is certainly a pre-COVID question.) I personally love the Duchess of Cambridge and her fascinators and hats. Princess Beatrice and Princess Eugenie? They need a fashion overhaul.

14. *Smiling at Strangers.* William Butler Yeats said, "Strangers are only friends you haven't yet met."

Before young Forrest Gump climbed his school bus steps for this first day of school and meeting the driver for the first time he said, "Mama said I should never be taking rides from strangers." The driver says, "This is the bus for school." Forrest answers, "I am Forrest. Forrest Gump." She responds, "I'm Dorothy Harris." He responds, "Now we ain't strangers anymore."

15. *Making Eye Contact.* You wouldn't want the person to think you don't like them at first meeting, do you? Wait until second meeting.

16. *Hospitality (having an Open Door policy).* Mi Casa es su Casa? When someone drops by unexpectedly, I go around apologizing for my lack of keeping a neat home. I should follow Erma Bombeck's theory, "If the item doesn't multiply, smell, catch fire, or block the refrigerator door, let it be." She says, "No one else cares. Why should you?"

17. *Helping your neighbors in times of happiness or sorrow.* This has been a tough one in COVID because normally I would offer food. I am afraid that now they might not want to eat something cooked in my kitchen if they are unsure about it origin. I am now offering a plant.

18. *RSVP.* You know what each letter stands for, right? It's *French.* I love French. It reads, *respondez s'il vous plait* or "respond if you please." Remember "please" popped up in part one of the manner list

19. *Hostess Gifts.* I am big on these because I know, as a hostess, the trouble one goes to clean up a home, prepare the food, and securing entertainment should

it be required. Why not make her day by making her smile? So what if the hostess doesn't like the gift. She can always re-gift. (Nowhere is there a rule for that one that I know.)

20. *Loyalty*. *Southern Living* defines this as "picking a side and sticking to it." They mention it is just another example of living up to your word. "Be loyal to your family, your friends, your sorority, your football team, your state, and your country." All I can add to that definition is "WOW!"

21. *No Gossiping*. By definition gossip is casual or "unconstrained conversation or reports about other people, typically involving details that are not confirmed as being true." It was Alice Roosevelt Longworth who said, "If you haven't got anything nice to say about anybody, come sit next to me."

22. *Avoid swearing in public*. According to the Tim Hawkins Handbook for Alternate Cuss Words, which has been field tested and mother approved, one can divide cussing into three categories: Alternate words to use when one is MIFFED (M), one is EXASPTERATED (E), and finally when one is NOT HAVING ANY OF IT (N). Ready?

M– shucks/E – Good Gravy/N –Great Googley Moogley.

M–Darn/E-Doggonit/N-H-E-Double-Hockey-Sticks

M –Phooey/E-Malarkey/N-What the What?

M-Shoot/E-Bucket-Head/N-Jumpin' Jehoshaphat

M-Dang/E-Confound It/N-Gee Willikers

If you'd like more creative swearing, research Tim Hawkins Handbook for Alternate Cuss Words.

Hop Dang Diggity

I found a new beer. It's an India Pale Ale but birthed in the South. Jekyll Island to be exact. According to the brewery's press, this Southern IPA "is brewed to remind us of the aroma of those tall Georgia pines, while the malty backbone balances everything out. Hopped up like a one-legged chicken, this ain't your standard IPA, Darlin."

Did I mention it was created in Georgia? That in itself is reason to give it a go.

And I love the name. It reminds me of Grandpa from "The Real McCoys" a 1950s/1960s television show. When grandpa Amos became so exasperated with his grandson, he'd say, "Dag Nab It, Luke!" Dag. Dang. Whatever.

What are some of the words and phrases we used to say to remind us of another time? My husband makes fun of me, dag nab it; I even make fun of me, too, when I catch myself wanting to watch a certain television show that I am not going to be able to see at the moment and ask him to please, "tape it for me." Another archaic television slang is, "Don't touch that dial" because we might miss the TV show where we learned to express how well things are going by saying we are, "…living the 'Life of Riley'" a show from 1953 – 1958. And speaking of television, I don't remember reading this but do remember hearing the commercial for Carter's Liver Pills. In 1868, Samuel J. Carter, of Erie, Pennsylvania, began peddling a pill he said could cure any type of stomach sickness. Within a generation, these "Carter's Little Liver Pills" could also cure headaches, constipation, and indigestion, according to Mr. Carter. So many pills! When one heard the phrase, something like, "You have more excuses than Carter has pills", you'd get it. But that phrase seems long gone, too.

Other media and technological expressions that hung around for a while but seem extinct are, "I'll see you in the funny papers", "You sound like a broken record", or "Carbon copy."

Today we may have Dollar Stores, but in my youth, we had Five and Dimes where we could purchase Mickey Mouse wristwatches, hula hoops, candy cigarettes, skate keys, little wax bottles of colored sugar water, those lips made of red wax, Bit of Honey candy, fireballs, and see an organ grinder's monkey. Outside the variety store there would be a dime-store pony for children to enjoy riding on and every kid had a chance to be Roy Rogers or Dale Evans, even though the ride only lasted sixty seconds.

Our style and attire? Gone are the ways of beehives. No more pedal pushers, poodle skirts, or saddle shoes. Phrases? "Knee-high to a grasshopper", "Fiddlesticks", "Cooties", "Going like sixty", "It don't take any wooden nickels", "Heaven to Murgatroyd", "Oh, my stars and garters!", and the phrase "Away we go!" taken from Jackie Gleason's comedy television show, "The Honeymooners".

Dances had names: the jerk, the smooth jerk, the frog, the 'gator, the twist, the peppermint twist, the hully gully, the Watusi, the fly, the pony, the stroll, the Freddie, not to forget doing the hand jive at sock hops.

And romance? Hubba-hubba! We'd go necking and smooching and spooning and cooing at some passion pit, lovers' lane, or rest area where we might end up with a hickey, passion mark, or suck bump. Gee Willikers! Jumpin'

Jehoshaphat! Heavens to Betsy! People that got on your nerves were knuckleheads, nincompoops, or pills.

There is plenty more nostalgia where these came from. If you would like to send a few of your own, you can reach me at lee@leestjohnauthor.com. I'd love to hear from you.

It's five o'clock somewhere and time to go. Saying goodbye has changed since newer phrases like "I'll be back" or "Hasta la vista, baby" superseded the one I still say on occasion, "See 'ya later, alligator." I'm off to drink a Hop, Dang, Diggity.

How Are Your Spirits?

Hubby and I found a new summertime five o'clock recipe. It is called a Cucumber, Basil, Lime Gimlet. Calling for gin, we substituted vodka. It must be low carb because vodka is one of the best liquors to have for counting out carbs and the cucumbers, basil, and limes have trace carbohydrates in them, so it is perfect for us and refreshing. The best part is no aftertaste, so you don't even know you are drinking vodka – until you do, if you know what I mean. (I would recommend drinking no more than two – see recipe below.)

Then my mind wondered to what other kind of mixed drinks could be served to satisfy the food pyramid in the nutritious vegetable and fruit group like cucumber and lime? This idea is to make sure we are eating healthy and at least *drinking* our vegetables. I looked up the best vegetables for digestion and The American Academy of Nutrition and Dietetics recommended: 1) apples with skin, 2) artichokes, 3) baked beans, 4) barley, 5) black beans, 6) bran flakes, 7) broccoli, 8) green beans, 9) green peas, 10) lentils, 11) lima beans, 12) pears with skin, 13) raspberries, 14) split peas, 15) turnip greens, and 16) whole wheat spaghetti. How many five o'clock drinks can be made with these choices? What aperitif can we find where you can drink your vegetables while enjoying the spirits?

1. There is already an Appletini.
2. Artichoke Manhattans – no joke.

3. Since I could not find an actual drink, we'll have to say hot dogs, hamburgers, and baked beans need to be washed down with beer. See #4

4. Most beers are made with barley.

5. Many Mexican dishes use black beans. That means margaritas and lime.

6. This is getting harder. But I found this: The use of wheat bran as a new adjunct in brewing at 25 % of total grist in combination with the use of a xylanase in the mashing step was tested by brewing control and bran-brewed lager beers.

7. They are calling these drinks cocktails, but they may be just smoothies. Just add vodka.

8. A Green Bean mixed drink? Oh, ye, of little faith. From Cocktail Builder: it contains 1 oz. orange juice and 3 oz. Hpnotiq liqueur. Whatever that is. Served without ice and garnish with vegetable of choice.

9. Pea and Cucumber Cooler.

10. Lentils – beans and more beans. Have a beer and then maybe some Gas-X.

11. Lima Beans – well, this one was tricky, and I found nothing.

12. Oh, there are lots of these and they mostly require bourbon.

13. Raspberries go well with gin, vodka, or rum.

14. What is the difference between split pea and peas? See #9

15. I found nothing. But see below regarding spinach.

16. Beer is brewed from cereal grains—most commonly from malted barley, though wheat, maize (corn), and rice are also used.

Since I couldn't find turnip greens you can do one of two things: a) substitute spinach for a papaya, spinach, coconut rum cocktail or b) throw those vegetables (like #11) that are not nestled in a mixed drink of their own into a Bloody Mary. You know that drink could have the kitchen sink in it.

But here is *our* new summer concoction and it's just five ingredients:

1 ½ basil, fresh leaves

2 slices cucumber

¼ oz. lime juice, fresh

1 ½ oz. vodka

1.You can muddle the basil and cucumber with a mortar and pestle, but a shaker will work just fine.

2. Add remaining ingredients and ice and shake.

3. Strain into a rocks glass over ice.

4. Garnish with a basil leaf.

Voila! A refreshing summer libation.

And although prunes were not on the list, I did look them up and found nothing. Although I guess you could make a prune martini with prune juice and your favorite go-to liquor.

Standing the Test of Time
1910s Chocolate Pie

My mother was born in 1913. When she was six years old, her mother succumbed to the 1919 Spanish Influenza. She and her younger brother were left in the care of the bottom tier of her mother's brothers and sisters: nine aunts and uncles. Her mother was in the top three of that chain of siblings. My grandfather was an alcoholic and unable to properly keep my mother and her four-year-old brother. So, they went to live with her mother's family.

That's a bunch of folks in the family home.

I heard that Aunt Jennie Jo was the matriarch of this brood. She never married and was the mother hen since their parents were gone. And, boy, could she cook! Well, looks like she had to with all those mouths to feed until some were married and moved on.

My mother followed and watched Aunt Jo, as they called her, whipping up meals for those still at home. I have kept all my mother's handwritten recipes in her original wooden recipe box, which I am sure many came from her aunt. They are a treasure trove of vintage, mid-century, and even modern dishes. She, too, loved to cook.

I researched 'recipes from the 1910s and 1920s' online and came across a Chocolate Pie recipe. You probably have seen it before as it was familiar to me, also. I am sharing my mother's version with you. Next time there is a celebration, this might be one you can make from scratch and have the taste and memories flood back from when your grandmother or mother might have made a similar one.

You will need a double boiler.

Ingredients for pie:

2 ½ cups milk

2 oz. unsweetened chocolate chopped

1/3 all-purpose flour

¼ cup milk

¼ tsp. salt

1/8 tsp. cinnamon

1 cup sugar

3 or 4 egg yolks

2 Tbs. butter

1 tsp. vanilla

½ cup chopped pecans

Pie shell

Directions:

Scald 2 ½ cup milk in double boiler. Cut up and add 2 oz. chocolate.

In separate bowl combine flour, ¼ cup milk, salt, cinnamon, and sugar. Add to double boiler's milk and chocolate then cook fifteen minutes. Pour small quantity over three or four egg yolks, beat, and then add mixture back to double boiler. Stir and cook for three minutes.

Add butter. Remove from heat and add vanilla and chopped nuts.

Let cool. Pour in pie shell.

Meringue Topping Ingredients:

• 2 large egg whites

• ½ cup sugar

• ¼ teaspoon cream of tartar or ½ teaspoon lemon juice

Directions:

Step 1: Beat egg whites

In a large bowl, combine egg whites with cream of tartar and beat until foamy. You can do this with a stand or hand mixer on medium or with a handheld whisk. (If you go the latter route, you'll get an arm workout, for sure.) Try not to overbeat the eggs at this point or they'll have a harder time combining with your sugar. Once the whites are foamy, kind of like soap bubbles, stop.

Step 2: Slowly add the sugar

Gradually add the sugar, 1 tablespoon at a time. Beat well after each addition to combine.

Step 3: Beat until stiff peaks form

Continue beating until stiff glossy peaks form. How can you tell it's right? Test by lifting the beater from the bowl. The peaks of the egg whites that rise as you lift should stand straight up, and the ones on the beaters should stick out too. Also, if you tilt the bowl, the whites should not slide. You shouldn't see any clear watery egg at the bottom. Double check to make sure the sugar is dissolved. Pinch some meringue between your fingers. It should feel silky smooth to the touch.

If you are finding yourself in the kitchen more these days, maybe you and your family will enjoy a vintage chocolate pie.

"Old Age Ain't No Place for Sissies"– Bette Davis

Before we both married, my good-friend-partner-in-crime and I would carry on and act like fools committing all sorts of shenanigans in the late 1970s and early 1980s. We both didn't marry until we were almost thirty, so that meant that we were putting off adulting as long as we could. Well, she grew up. I never did.

About a decade ago, I was spending the night with her while her husband was out of town and we went out to dinner in a rather lovely restaurant in Sandy Springs near where she lives. I must have been in a jovial mood as I was having fun speaking in the English dialect I use during some of my speaking engagements even today. I mean, I am pretty good at this accent to even fool some of the English-born who have moved to Georgia.

I was acting proper while trying to prank the waitress with this dialect. An inside joke. But when the waitress left, my friend told me I couldn't act like that anymore. I needed to be respectable. After all, I guess it was because I was in ATLANTA. She wanted me to behave. Say what? When did she grow old? When did she lose her sense of fun? Why did it matter if I acted silly? No one but us knew, and yet, I was embarrassing her.

We are still good friends but I see now she is taking life seriously and I am not. Oh, I have my moments for serious discussions and actions, but really? This wasn't one of those serious times.

I remember my mother saying, "Getting old ain't for sissies." Well, I see now that Bette Davis said it best. And I know what she meant was the aging process. But can it not also be interpreted as to how you look at life?

On page S6 of the *Atlanta Journal-Constitution* on Wednesday, March 5, 2003, there was an article called PRIMETIME/VOICES titled, "The Wisdom of Aging". I kept it all these years to solidify my point of view about aging. Here are the quotes from that article:

"You don't stop laughing because you grow old. You grow old because you stop laughing." – Michael Pritchard, speaker/humorist.

"Though it sounds absurd, it is true to say I felt younger at 60 than I felt at 20." – Ellen Glasgow, writer/poet.

"The longer I live, the more beautiful life becomes." – Frank Lloyd Wright, architect.

"It is a mistake to regard age as a downhill grade toward dissolution. The reverse is true. As one grows older, one climbs with surprising strides." – George Sand, writer.

"At 20 years of age, will reigns; at 30, the wit; at 40, the judgment." – Benjamin Franklin (*maybe this is what my friend was talking about*).

"Forty is the old age of youth; fifty, the youth of old age. – Victor Hugo, poet/novelist (*now that's more like it!*)

"We grow neither better or worse as we get old, but more like ourselves." – May L. Becker, editor.

"We are not limited by our old age; we are liberated by it." – Stu Mittleman, runner

"What I still ask for daily – for life as long as I have work to do and work as long as I have life." – Reynolds Price, author.

"The quality, not the longevity, of one's life is what is important." – The Rev. Martin Luther King, Jr., civil rights leader.

"Grow old along with me! The best is yet to be, the last of life, for which the first was made." – Robert Browning, poet.

"By the time we hit 50, we have learned our hardest lessons. We have found out that only a few things are really important. We have learned to take life seriously, but never ourselves." – Marie Dressler, actress.

And my personal favorite…

"Middle age is when you've met so many people that every new person you meet reminds you of someone else." – Ogden Nash.

Becoming Your Parents

Have you seen the Progressive Insurance commercial that confesses they can't help protecting you from becoming your parents, but they can protect your home and auto if you bundle your insurance plan with them? My favorite commercial, "Donpeldinner", shows a couple moving into a new house and the wife begins to see a change in her husband, Rich. When Rich's parents come for a visit, the wife is enlightened after she observes Rich's mannerisms and notices that he acts exactly like his mother.

If you are of a certain age, do you see yourself turning into your parents? These commercials ring true to me. I am of that age. Here are some clues that you and I have crossed over becoming them and we didn't even see it coming. "Oh, no! I'll never!" we thought. Well, get ready to see if you can check off some of these observations about your new (old) self.

If you find you are watching more of the Discovery Channel than you used to, you've crossed over. I can come into a room to watch a television show I like to find that from the previous night when hubby was watching television the channel is on the aforementioned channel.

And speaking of appreciating nature, I bet you never really stopped and watched all the birds in your yard. Now when one is close, you stop and admire it and think about the beauty of nature all around you. You might be turning into your parents with that one. Before you were too busy to stop and notice for any length of time, but now that you are retired or reflective, you, too, go through this bird phase.

Another clue is while catching up on news or celebrity gossip on your computer, or in the magazines at your hairdresser's, or maybe even your nail salon, you come across more than a dozen names of new/young celebrities you have never heard of. You don't even recognize their faces. It's just another world out there where you don't know who these people are and why they are even important.

Although forty-five years removed from college graduation, I still help out with my sorority by writing letters of recommendation for applicants to my sorority. All these years I've filled out hand-written information about the young lady wanting to go through my sorority's rush at several universities in the Southeast. Our national magazine always had a copy on the last page of the quarterly publication but since the magazine has gone digital, it's not there and I am supposed to go through a portal to retrieve that recommendation form to fill out. I suppose I can do it on-line or copy and paste and fill it in the old school way, but I can't even retrieve it because I can't get in the portal. HELP!

Been house hunting lately? Or dreaming of the day when you want to down-size and especially find a home that doesn't have stairs because you want your master bedroom on the main level? You probably saw your parents go through this, too. My husband and I are idiots as we did the reverse. We always lived in a ranch, like our parents, and recently bought an historic home where all the bedrooms are upstairs. But don't think we haven't already decided where the elevator is going.

And who of us from a certain age hasn't planned an outing where we take into consideration leaving wherever the outing is to make certain we leave the venue before the traffic buildup from everyone leaving at once? Don't tell me you haven't considered that idea and maybe even implemented it.

Yes, Progressive Insurance knows us well.

If I Could Turn Back Time

We gained an hour on November 4th so what did I do with that extra time I was given? I'll tell you how productive I was.

1. I watched my dog stare at me around his previous night's dinner time. His internal clock told him it was time to eat but with this juncture, we were going to have to change all that. I would be starting a new routine like we do every time change. This fall, again, I was going to delay feeding him five minutes from the preceding night to push the meal back little by little to the new time. It's going to take at least twelve days to make up that hour and it is almost unbearable to observe my dog staring at me until he is fed. 5 minutes.

2. I went around my house setting all my clocks to the correct time although what was the point? I always look at my phone for the time anyway. 10 minutes.

3. I tried to figure out how to set my sundial in my garden back an hour. After a few minutes, I gave up. 5 minutes.

4. My dog let me know he needed to go out, but it was later than before because of the return to Eastern Standard Time. I was able to get fifteen more minutes of sleep than I normally would. Even then, I held off as long as I could before taking him out but then he became anxious about going outside to do his business by going around in circles on my

comforter waking me up even more to let me know it was time! 15 minutes.

5. While lying in bed before having to stave off the dog, I tried to figure out Daylight Savings Time in general. 7 minutes.

6. Forgetting to change the time-controlled coffee maker the night before, I had to reprogram it for the coffee maker to turn on. 3 minutes.

7. I woke up during the night to go to the bathroom and it took me at least five minutes to fall back asleep after each trip. Three Xs 5 = 15 minutes.

So, that's what I did with my extra hour of time: nothing of importance.

There are some good points:

1. If you never changed your clock in your car last spring, your time will finally be correct.

2. And with that said, you may just want to keep your microwave clock the same rather than try to search for the instructions manual on how to change the time. Looking for that manual is frustrating and is that time well spent?

3. My smart phone must be smart. It set the new time itself.

4. Watching the movie, "Back to the Future" has new meaning now.

"I love the end of fall when it gets dark by 4 p.m.," said no one ever.

This time change, especially concerning Central Standard Time, is one reason I would not let my husband move me to Alabama. It's worse over there.

Over the Moon

A year ago, there was some big hoopla going around about seeing some special moon that only is visible every few decades, but I don't remember the specific name for that phenomena. There are so many types of moons I am supposed to be looking for, I can't keep up.

There are many lovely sentiments that go with the word 'moon'. I love the expression, "I love you to the moon and back." I also love this book, "Love You Forever". It doesn't have anything to do with a moon; I just like it. One reason I like it is because of the cover. There is a two-year-old sitting on the floor of a bathroom next to a toilet with toilet paper all off its roll and all over him. This toddler is just so proud of himself holding up some strips of the paper high above his head.

That cover was once my life. Bathroom humor – it's a double entendre, you know. Having only sons, I had to make some major adjustments in life such as "going along to get along" in this male-dominated family - laughing instead of getting really grossed out. Maybe I even became used to it.

Yes, I am trying to make a point.

One of my girlfriends is a flight attendant and was on a layover somewhere in Europe at one of their nude beaches. Mind you, she wasn't nude. While lying in her lounge chair she sent me a close-up picture of a moon. Yes, a moon. Not the one in the sky but the one that boys (and some girls) don't mind showing you. She knew I'd laugh because, well, it's bathroom humor and I'd become accustomed.

If you are not familiar with the term mooning, let me catch you up. Mooning is the recreational act of baring one's bottom in public with the intention of it being seen by people who don't want, or expect, to see it. Boys are probably more often baring their buttocks than girls. Why do I say that? It's a one step process with males. They can drop their drawers and their trousers with one sweep. Girls, and notice I did not say ladies, will usually have to pull up their dress and then drop their drawers. The moment to shock might be lost in the two-step process.

Because the exposed moon on a beach full of tourists is not seen very often in America, my girlfriend decided to send me the sight she was seeing while sitting on that beach. It wasn't very pretty. And this was about the time of whenever some much-ballyhooed moon event was taking place in 2018. With my warped sense of humor from hanging out with all the males in my house, I shared on a closed community of humorists on Facebook this beach beauty's rompos pompus. I used her and her thong as my backdrop with this saying "They told me to take a picture of the moon, but I guess I took the wrong one."

And, boy, did I get a backlash. I thought I was making a funny about the literal word, moon, and its urban dictionary definition. The readers were upset that I was body-shaming this female because of her oversize body and that strip on her backside she called a thong.

Where did that jump come from? I didn't even know what body-shaming was until it was mentioned on-line. I guess I should have but because her body size was not my target, just her derriere, I was taken aback as they bullied me to take it down. I did.

Is mooning only a Southern thing? I think not. But then again, I was wrong in thinking I was making a funny play on words.

Stupid is as Stupid Does
New York Version

…or so says Forrest Gump.

There is even a course for college credit entitled, STUPIDITY. *Description*: What better topic to rail against at college than stupidity? This course examines it at depth from literary, social, and philosophical perspectives. Offered at Occidental College, a nationally renowned liberal arts college integrating the cultural and intellectual resources of Los Angeles. Oh, that explains it. Even with a course like this, "You can't fix stupid."

Even worse, there are *still* blue laws on the books that show up which appear stupid today.

But first …why are they called Blue Laws? Many reference books say that the laws were called "blue" because they were first printed on blue paper. However, historians have said that the term is more likely to be derived from the use of the word "blue" to mean "rigidly moral" and date back to first prohibiting activities on Sundays under the reign of Roman Emperor, Constantine in the year 321.

New Yorkers are still saddled with dozens of anachronistic laws that today seem staggeringly stupid. It's easy to pass laws regulating people's behavior but is very difficult to repeal those laws. Among the city and state's lamest laws:

1. *It is against the law to throw a ball at someone's face.* A person is guilty of "offensive exhibition" if

75

they operate a public event where a person is "voluntarily submitting to indignities such as the throwing of balls…at one's head or body." The law's origin appears to protect carnies from abusive bosses. Other sections outlaw "propelling" knives at a person or making them ride a bike or dance "without respite for more than 8 hours."

2. *It is illegal to sell cat or dog hair.* A statute that's part of the state's anti-cruelty provisions makes it a crime to "import, sell, offer for sale…transport or otherwise market" dog or cat fur. But guess what you can traffic? Coyote, fox, lynx, or bobcat fur.

3. *Flirting can result in a $25 fine.* Flutter your eye lashes with flirtatious intent and be prepared to cough up 25 bucks. This is why this statute can only be from the north. This behavior has Southern DNA written all over it. This mannerism would have the jails below the Mason-Dixon line so overcrowded with flirtatious females because we've been trained at an early age to flirt.

4. *A license must be purchased before hanging clothes on a clothesline.* If cops ever cracked down on this law, half of Brooklyn would be in jail. However, luckily many states are revoking this band because this once sight for sore eyes is now considered to be eco-friendly. Lucky you, Alabama.

5. *No taking selfies with tigers.* Say what? Well, since 2014 this law has been on the books with a $500 fine to prevent people being mauled since there were two in the last ten years when the public was allowed to

cozy up to big cats because of county fairs or when traveling circuses came to town.

6. *It's against the law to run a puppet show in a window.* I know you'd want to, but don't even think about it. $25 fine and 30 days in jail.

7. *You may not walk around on Sundays with an ice cream cone in your pocket.* Theoretically, sweet-toothed outlaws would pocket their vanilla cones to hide them from passing policemen. This idea is so uncomfortable I can't mock it any more than what it already is.

And this is why I started this topic:

8. *It's illegal for two or more mask-wearing people to congregate in public.* This law has been in existence since 1845 "when tenant farmers, in response to a lowering of wheat prices, dressed up" as Native Americans and "covered their faces with masks in order to attack the police anonymously."

I don't think they are enforcing this penal code in New York.

Stupid is as Stupid Does
Georgia Version

Last chapter, I wrote about New York's idiotic laws still in the books. This chapter is Georgia's turn. People have been living in Georgia since it was founded as an English Colony in 1773 and that means there are Georgia laws that potentially date back that far. Even though we may not know the origins of some of these laws, here are a few where you might either get a giggle or realize you are breaking a few without knowing it.

1. Gainesville, Georgia has an ordinance that requires you to eat fried chicken with your hands. Passed in 1961, it was a publicity stunt to promote Gainesville's poultry industry. How could anyone enforce that today, you say? Well, in 2009 a 91-year-old woman visiting from Louisiana was arrested and charged with violating the ordinance. However, as luck would have it, Gainesville's mayor was on hand to pardon her. The whole event was a practical joke organized by a friend of hers for her 91st birthday. Were you way ahead of me and thinking that was going to happen?

2. Acworth, Georgia's residents are legally required to own a rake. Of course, the law doesn't add that it is needed to be used once in a while in their yards. Would a rake be considered a weapon?

3. In Athens – Clarke County, it's illegal to make a disturbing sound at a fair. What kind of disturbing

78

sound? My all-boy family makes disturbing sounds all the time. Does that mean we will have to circumvent Clarke County when we are traveling Northeast to the Georgia mountains? If we don't and we travel through the county, may I make a citizen's arrest should I hear that sound from one of them?

4. It's also a misdemeanor to keep a disorderly house. I guess I better not try to enforce #3 as they may turn the tables on me with this one.

5. Quitman, Georgia has made it illegal for chickens to cross the road. I guess those chickens will never fulfill their destiny or prophecy in the joke about them. Maybe the town was tired of seeing poultry owners' chickens not in their own yards and visitors making comments about that singular joke.

6. Atlanta prohibits vaudeville performers from rendering "coarse jokes". Well, first of all, who will define COARSE? And secondly, vaudeville? How old is this law?

7. In Marietta, it's illegal to spit in a public building. Never knew Marietta had such a problem. Are visitors to the buildings still chewing 'tabbackie'? Are there not spittoons?

8. *It is illegal to keep a donkey in a bathtub.* This one breaks my heart. Think of all the donkey lovers out there that might even use these animals as service animals. If they live with them in the house, how else are they going to keep them clean? If they cleaned them outside, they'd get dirty again in no time just walking across the yard toward the house.

9. *In Athens-Clarke County, Adult bookstores may not sell alcohol.* Wait a minute. Adult bookstores? Where are these adult bookstores? No, really, tell me. But in the meantime, what are the stores worried about with alcohol sales? Like teenagers, these so called "adults", having a few sips of inhibitors, might hide in the back section of the store and...

10. *Also in Athens-Clarke County, If you want to read your favorite book in public to your friends, do it before 2:45 AM.* Ok, so if you were thrown out of the adult bookstore because your brought your own "inhibitor" you could still buy a book before you leave. However, big brother is watching if you are reading that purchase after 2:45 a.m. anywhere in public with your "friend" who left with you.

11. *Athens-Clarke County -- Goldfish may not be given away to entice someone to enter a game of bingo.* They didn't say Goldfish crackers, did they? Who doesn't love those cheesy crackers? Every time I play bridge or bunco, there are bowls of goodies to munch on including goldfish crackers. They need to make this law clearer.

12. *Persons under the age of 16 may not play pinball after 11:00 PM in Athens-Clarke County.* And yet the pre-teens are the fastest pinball wizards! They aren't going to bed at 11:00 p.m. anyway. Now they are going to have to go out and find something else keep their adrenaline up after a game of pinball and we were all told nothing good happens after 11:00 p.m. Just let them play! At least we know where they are.

13. *If you're going out of business in Athens-Clarke County, you will need a business license to hold a going-out-of-business sign.* How stupid is this? How else will people know you are going out of business? And this county houses students attending the University of Georgia where there are supposedly lots of smart people living.

14. *In Athens-Clarke County it is illegal to sell two beers for the price of one.* I doubt anyone in Clarke County is enforcing this one.

15. *Owners of mules may not allow their animal to roam around Athens unsupervised.* What if they were given a bath outside like the donkeys and got loose? Mules can run as fast as forty miles an hour under certain conditions. These poor mule owners…fined for keeping them in your house or fined for having them outside to break away. Maybe one shouldn't be a mule owner.

Or maybe one shouldn't live in Athens.

Are these laws something we should be wary of and worried about today? Are these considered first-world problems? You know what first world problems are, right? They are relatively trivial or minor problems or frustrations (implying a contrast with serious problems such as those that may be experienced in the developing world). But as we've heard, it's easier to make a law than it is to retrieve it from existence.

Think of all the pork barrel legislation that goes on. *Pork barrel* is a metaphor for the appropriation of government spending for localized projects secured solely or primarily to bring money to a representative's district. The usage originated in American English. Scholars use it as a technical term regarding legislative control of local appropriations.

Do we know what is in those pork barrel projects being accepted under our noses? They might just be crazy like any one of the above *or* in the doozies next week. Stay tuned.

I am Karen. Hear Me Roar

It seems there is a new pejorative term used in the United States and other English-speaking countries for a woman perceived as entitled. She is demanding beyond the scope of what is appropriate or necessary. The common stereotypical woman is white and who uses her privilege to demand her own way at the expense of others. You might know her (or yourself) when you hear (or say) her demand to "speak to the manager". Other negative characteristics of this woman is she has anti-vaccination beliefs, racist, or sports a particular hairstyle (a bob). In 2020, the term used to describe this woman is increasingly being used as a general-purpose term of disapproval for a middle-aged white woman.

The name for this stereotype woman? KAREN. Hopefully it didn't seem as though I *partially* behaved like one the other day in the supermarket. The only descriptions in a KAREN that might apply to me are my age, the color of my skin, and my haircut. Oh, and I asked to see the manager of the store. Well, I didn't actually ask for the manager but a partner in crime did and she looked like me, too.

Let me explain.

I drove from Newnan to Peachtree City's Fresh Market because of the advertisement for one of their meal deals. This particular meal contained four boneless pork chops, a side of mashed potatoes, a side of mixed vegetables, chipotle sauce, and half an apple pie all for twenty dollars. It was sixteen dollars off! So, the twenty-mile drive was worth it and I go once a week anyway, mostly on Tuesdays.

But when I arrived, they were out of boneless pork chops and chipotle sauce. While standing at the meat counter and finding they did have a few bone-in chops, I was considering buying them that way. A woman beside me in line (we were wearing masks) was as dumbfounded as I was about not finding what was advertised. If they were out, could they not offer us a ticket to come back another time and find the product like other grocery stores do when they are sold out?

The gal next to me was more in a tizzy than I was as she was counting on serving this already prepared dinner to guests that evening. We began identifying with each other's plight. We both saw the bone-in pork chops and I heard her say to the butcher, "Is it possible to put together another meal with these pork chops in your case?" I chirped in, "I'd like that, too!"

Of course he didn't know if that was allowed. We probably both said at the same time, "May we see your manager?" After a few moments of discussion with the manager, *we got our wish*, and they put together another meal for us with bone-in chops. But, uh-oh, they were out of the chipotle sauce that would make this meal more delectable and because there were no more on their shelves either, nor this flavor by another company, we had to have help deciding from which new sauce to add to this meal and keep within the same cost of the 'meal deal of the day'.

The other KAREN and I received help to pull it all together and we were very happy. And why not? We kept on keeping on until we got our way. Although we were very pleasant with the Fresh Market associates and they were very helpful meeting our needs, we certainly didn't stop trying to be creative with solving our problem. In other words, I think we were pushy.

So, I'd like to write this letter to the kind folks at Peachtree City Fresh Market:

Dear Fresh Market,

My new acquaintance and I are most appreciative for you help and service to create a new variation of your pork chop Meal Deal of the Day. Thank you for taking care of us.

Sincerely,

Karen

Where Shopping is a Pleasure

Uh, I don't think so and I don't just mean Publix. I think many people will agree with me. Shopping is dull these days. You men out there might not get it because men go shopping to buy what they *want* but women go shopping to find out *what* they want and there isn't much to find out there.

Before you even reach a store, just the idea of shopping is depressing knowing what you must deal with. If able, one has to protect oneself shopping in person by going during hours when fewer people will be there like early morning or late at night. Even then the shopping is not pleasurable.

This is the kind of stuff you find:

1. Craving spaghetti? The only box of noodles left is made of chickpeas. Gross. And it's angel hair. Just the kind you wanted. But here is a hint – if pasta is unavailable in the spaghetti section of your store, try the Italian section. Maybe you'll get lucky. NOT!

2. Craving cereal? You have choices here: Raisin Bran, Shredded Wheat, and Special K.

3. Craving specialty pizza? At Trader Joe's they have frozen kale. That's all and that is what makes it special. If you aren't shopping at Trader Joe's, there are lots of cauliflower frozen pizzas. YUM! Your favorite, I'm sure.

4. If cauliflower or kale aren't to your liking, you can still eat your vegetables because there are plenty of beets, lima beans, chocolate hummus, and turnips. Better hurry up before they are all gone!

5. Getting hungry reading this? You'll find cream of bacon soup in the soup aisle. Who knew this even existed?

6. What to drink? Flax milk is stocked full. Not only is there a lot of Corona beer, it has been marked *way down*. Might want to get some to relieve your tension because everyone else bought the stress relief tea.

7. Looking for meat? The only thing available is either gristly blade steak or enormous porterhouse steaks. The cheapest cut *and* the most expensive. Literally nothing in between. Well, maybe. Check out the frozen section for faux meat products. Or you might find six or ten pounds of pork chitterlings.

8. Are you still looking for toilet paper? Don't be fooled. There are boxes of old Halloween candy stuffed into the toilet paper section. At a distance it looks like that section has been restocked. But once you get closer, you see there is no treat. Just a trick. But there is hope! At some Wal-Mart stories there are still plenty of Dude Wipes stocked on the shelf. Yep, the manly man butt wipes. I guess even in a pandemic there is a line one doesn't cross.

9. And here in the South, there is even a bigger trick. All the Duke's mayo is gone and all that is left is Hellmann's.

Don't forget there are the arrows in the supermarkets telling you which way to walk so don't you dare go up the down aisle or go down the up aisle. People will give you stares, and the stares stand out because the rest of their faces are behind masks. I finally became so frustrated having to circle around again. If I passed the shelf of the item I forgot to get to the first time, I now either walk backwards with my cart in tow as though I am facing the right way of the pointing arrow or I leave my buggy at the end of the aisle and head back to the shelf I missed to retrieve the item. Why did I miss it in the first place? They were *out of stock!*

And if you are like me and the frustration of finding a food item is getting to you, head to Chick-Fil-A where every time you thank them for taking your order, they respond with, "My pleasure."

At least someone is taking pleasure when it comes to buying and selling food.

The grocery store is becoming more like a medical office. Everything is sterilized, people are wearing masks, and yesterday the clerk gave me my annual breast exam.

Yes, those annoying masks. Everyone looks almost downtrodden. Most everyone keeps to themselves and there is no lively spontaneous conversation any more in the supermarkets. Of course, some people may like that. I like to chat sometimes with people. I used to be cornered in the grocery store by the parents of the children I taught to get the 411 on how their child was doing in school. I guess masks pretty much prevent these that these days.

Do you wear one?

They are touted as having good qualities in today's viral world but what are some of the drawbacks of wearing a mask? This is what I have noticed when wearing one. You decide which of the following would fit in either category: good qualities or drawbacks-

1. Men on the street no longer tell me to smile. I don't have to. FREEDOM!
2. While in the school building, students could use their mask as a cheat sheet during a test.
3. If you wear a mask to the grocery store, it disguises you when you are purchasing obscene amounts of junk food.
4. Why purchase a brand-new mask? You could just use one of your bras.
5. The mask hooks behind your ears where you can carry your sunglasses, headphones, etc. Your ears are your new purse.
6. I can mouth bad words, and no one notices.
7. I bought the super-duper extreme, three-lined, top shelf, most protection for the price mask online from the HAVE NO FEAR shop. I made sure it was NOT made in China. According to my scale my face mask weighs 6 pounds.
8. You can burp and the sound is muffled. However, if you notice people dropping like flies, it's probably because of having to smell one's own morning breath.
9. In 2010, according to a nonscientific test done by MythBusters sneezing into your elbow can affectively prevent the fluids from spreading. So, do I remove my mask when I sneeze into my sleeve? What is the correct etiquette for that these days?
10. Speaking of mask etiquette, should couples wear masks? I keep seeing where the woman is wearing a face mask and the man isn't, even in grocery stores.

11. Another etiquette question: why do people alone in their cars wear a mask? Should joggers wear them? (Remember, they too are breathing in their own morning breath.)

12. While shopping in public, should a shopper train their children to loudly ask, why isn't that person wearing a mask? Are we going to get sick? Some parents tell me this is COVID parenting tip #3.

13. Here is the best feeling while having worn a mask all day in public: ripping off your mask when you get back in the car is the new taking off your bra when you get home.

And where is the Muzak once found in the grocery store? You know about Muzak, don't you? It's a term used for most forms of background music and sometimes called "life music" because it is thought it would give a lift to buyers to spend more while shopping. Before it often seemed irritating. But now that shopping isn't a pleasure and most patrons seem sour and dour, I miss it. Especially any song by Earth, Wind, and Fire.

Numbers Game

A Facebook friend was involved in a quandary, needed answers to her dilemma, and wrote this on Facebook recently: "Does anyone in the Facebook world know the four-digit produce code for bananas? I am trying to prove that my husband is a weirdo for knowing this number. I bought organic bananas, but since my husband thinks it's ridiculous to spend money on organic things, I took off the stickers on the bananas. There was one sticker that wouldn't come off, so I at least got the word 'organic' off. There was still a produce code showing and *I got caught*.

He (raising his voice from the kitchen): 'Why did you buy organic bananas?'

Me (sitting and smiling, not saying anything but eventually gave up and asked): 'How did you know?'

He: 'Because regular bananas produce code is 4011 and these bananas start with a 9.'

Me: 'Who even knows that or would even pay attention to that?'"

And then she questioned her Facebook friends asking if they, too, either thought this weird or was it normal to know produce codes.

You know those little stickers on fruits and vegetables? They are called 'PRICE LOOK-UP' or PLUs. These codes contain numbers that cashiers use to ring up these kinds of purchases. But you can also use them to make sure you're getting what you paid for. Here is a clue of what to look for:

1. A five-digit number that starts with a 9 means it is *organic*.

2. A four-digit code beginning with a 3 or 4 means the produce is probably conventionally grown. Example: regular small lemons sold in the U.S. are labeled 4033; large are 4053; small organic lemons are coded 94033, large are 94053.

3. A five-digit code that starts with an 8 means the item is genetically modified (it has genes from other organisms).

What if PLUs overtook us in the future? I can see it now: Year: 2038 A.D.

"Hello?"

"Yes, hello. Is this Y. Bother Grocery?

"It is. May I help you?"

"Yes. I am calling to see if your shipment of 4011s arrived today? I wanted to make sure before I came over."

"Yes, ma'am. And our 94011s also arrived."

"Thank you. My husband only wants the 4011 variety."

"We will be having a sale next week if you can wait a week."

"What is on sale THIS week? I also need 4159. Are they still in season, too?"

"No, not those, but we have all the rest – 4082, 4663, 4665. Need those?"

"Of course. Doesn't everyone? May I ask you about more fruit? I think I saw some beautiful plump and juicy 4012s from Florida. Do you still have those?"

"We do. Our 4288s also came from Florida. They are just as juicy. If you are going to make any pies for the upcoming holidays, remember our 4240s, 4045s, and 4404s. They'll make your pies delicious."

"Any 4247s?"

"Did I not mention those? Yes ma'am. Certainly, have plenty of 'em."

"Thank you for your time. You have been so nice to give me all this information over the phone. What is your name?"

"My last name is Licious. D. Licious."

Who is the grocery shopper in your household and do you or they know these PLU codes? Test it out.

4011 – Banana
94011 – Organic Banana
4159 – Vidalia Onion
4082 – Red Onion
4663 – White Onion
4665 – Yellow Onion
4012 - Orange
4288 - Grapefruit
4240 - Blueberry
4045 - Cherry
4404 - Peach
4247 - Strawberry

Well, if it ain't Murphy ...

My husband and I are selling our lake condo. Everything about it is grand - from the two-story cathedral ceiling in the living room, two swimming pools (one was an infinity pool), assigned boat slip, but it is the water view that was the biggest attraction of all when we purchased. *And there are elevators.*

I used to be deathly afraid of them. Over time, I consciously overcame my fear by taking other building's elevators by myself now and then. What helped during my struggles in the 1980s and 1990s was to carry a purse with me onto these lifts. In my purse I had my checkbook. I was terrible when it came to keeping up with my check balancing. That's why I married an accountant. I thought, should the elevator get stuck and to keep me from freaking out, I would have plenty of time to balance my own checkbook. It never happened, but I was ready and that put me at ease.

I am still afraid of bridges. Not the low Chattahoochee Bridge-kind, but the high curved-kind like the bridge over the Savannah River. My overactive imagination wanders and that I might lose control of the steering wheel which would have a mind of its own and eventually steer itself over to the bridge railings and dangle there. Watching too many movies about that sort of thing, I guess.

Even with our condo's elevators, I carried on pretty well, although rarely going alone. Irrational as it was, I sometimes felt most comfortable taking the stairs from the third floor as getting stuck was always in the back of my mind because our elevator was temperamental. Many in our building had gotten trapped no matter how many times they 'fixed' it.

But Murphy was waiting for me.

Hubby was playing more golf and had already joined Still Waters Golf Club which meant he came over to the lake more than I did. Yes, we were still boating; yes, we had that grand water view, but we were of the age to downsize…and separate ourselves (me) from *those temperamental elevators*!

We purchased a ground floor level design. It is not directly on the water (has a view) but it is in the Still Waters Golf and Country Club Resort compound. That means it has a marina and boat lift for our boat - let them do all the work! We can just pull in or out without effort. No trailering the boat back to storage. Great for our age. Especially no more elevators to contend with. Wouldn't it be wonderful to leave before anything bad happened?

But it was not meant to be. Murphy must have found out about our last weekend there to remove a bit more furniture. I guess he learned about how many times I dog-cussed his involvement with our elevators. That last weekend I took the chance of running back out to our truck by myself to get a bag I had left when we unloaded. Coming up to the third floor, both doors started to open, but then decided not to open all the way and closed. There were instructions on the inside walls not to keep punching the floor buttons as it would hinder the doors *eventually* opening on their own.

I didn't freak except for wondering who was going to hear me yelling, or who was going to figure out, "Where is mama?" I started pounding on the door for help. It started to get warm. Finally, children playing nearby heard me and ran for assistance. My family came to keep me company while calling the maintenance supervisor. My retrieved travel bag contained – no, not a checkbook - but a crossword puzzle – *large print edition* – which kept me occupied while maintenance worked for thirty minutes until I was safe!

I conquered my fear of my mind playing tricks on me by keeping it busy, but I couldn't stop Murphy from laying down his Law.

I'll Show You!
(*Lesson One in 'Intolerance'*)

I have long been fascinated with the impetus of what causes some to achieve greatness. There are different definitions in one's mind of what greatness actually is. I think it is up to each individual to decide on who has achieved importance or distinction in a field. But once there, what was their motivation?

I remember reading about a young man while in middle school who was told by his principal that he would never amount to anything. That young man grew up to be Sam Massell, mayor of Atlanta from 1970 – 1974. First, that was an awful thing to say to a young child, in my opinion, and I have never read that statement put a fire under Sam's belly, but let's say it did.

Here's a true story that fascinated me. Have you been told you weren't worthy and yet you were able to prove you were?

This young man grew up in Boston, Massachusetts. All four of his grandparents had immigrated in the 1840s to escape the Irish famine. Born into a highly sectarian society where Irish Catholics were excluded by upper-class Boston Brahmins, he had a high-achieving father who left a legacy of established political and business wealth.

He was popular, good-looking, athletic, and intelligent. He was encouraged to work hard and set his sights high. He quickly began to make a name for himself, excelling at baseball. With all these talents, he began his career at

Harvard continuing his success and was included in the social stratosphere of exclusive social clubs.

Except for one: the male-only final club, the Porcellian Club, founded in 1791.

Freshmen could join a freshman club, then a "waiting club", and when students neared the end of their studies, a "final club." The "final clubs" were so named because they were the last social club a student would join before graduation and the Porcellian, according to a history of Harvard, is "the most final of them all."

Past members have included James Russell Lowell, both Oliver Wendell Holmeses, Henry Cabot Lodge, President Theodore Roosevelt, among other notables.

This student, successful in high school, thought Harvard to be no different. But in reality, it was. Being Porcellian Club material was not just another club where all of those outstanding traits and jovial personality like this student's would provide good fellowship for the other club members during their college years, it was whether one came from the right family and the right school, of being drawn from the same station of life. Those that were chosen had to have the similarity of past association and experiences because they were to be partners for years to come.

Because of his prestigious friends, he thought once he was accepted, he'd be set for life in distinguished brokerage houses and such. For weeks there had been avid speculation over who would be included in the elite seven final clubs. Nothing in his life's experiences had prepared him for what was about to happen.

As soon as its new members were chosen, the entire membership would march together through the streets of

Boston to hand deliver those treasured invitations while all anxiously waited in their rooms for that tap on the door. For Joseph P. Kennedy, Sr. it never came.

Joe had remained in his quarters as the hours slipped by. He shared his roommate's excitement as he was selected into one of the seven clubs. But by the end of the afternoon, he was forced to acknowledge that no one was coming. Not knowing how to respond, being blackballed because he was Catholic, and his future doors being closed to him, Joseph Kennedy redirected his energies to become a successful businessman, investor, and politician known for his high-profile positions in the United States government and for his political and other achievements of his children.

He did it his way and it was all because, as its Porcellian tradition dictated, that no Harvard man who was not a member could ever step across the threshold into that other exclusive privileged world.

(*Lesson Two in 'Intolerance'*)

Here's another true story that fascinated me. Have you been told you weren't worthy and yet you were able to prove you were?

I like mavericks. One of my favorite authors was one. This winner of the 1937 Pulitzer Prize for Fiction was as unorthodox as they came in the 1920's. She was an average college student and did not excel in any of her academics. She also had a taste for mischief.

She was a working woman at a time when women didn't work that much and decided to pursue a career in journalism.

She began writing as a reporter for the Atlanta Journal, where she received almost no encouragement from her family or "society."

She was flamboyant, wild, and unrestrained, but because of her family's standing in Atlanta, she debuted in 1920 for the Atlanta Junior League. She and her friend, a Georgia Tech student, delivered a sensational performance during the ball at the Georgia Terrace Hotel. The dance was called the Apache and was a provocative Parisian street dance of the Jazz age. One shocked Victorian matron declared, "I thought this was supposed to be an Indian dance! Did you see how he kissed her?" After her scandalous debut, she was denied membership into the Junior League.

She collected erotic Parisian postcards. She smoked. She drank. She married. She divorced. She remarried. Editor of New York's Macmillan Publishing, Harold Latham, visited Atlanta in 1935 in search of new authors. He had been told this thirty-five-year-old well-known journalist was working on a novel. Asking about its progress, the novelist denied its existence, although she had been working on it for nine months. The two parted company.

By chance, the author overheard a remark that evening that changed the course of history. "Imagine, anyone as silly as Margaret writing a book!" said one friend. That's all the goading Mitchell needed. She chased down Latham and plunked her unfinished manuscript into his hands. *Gone with the Wind* was the top American fiction bestseller in 1936 and 1937. Despite it being in the midst of the Great Depression, *Gone with the Wind* went on to sell one million copies in the first six months and today more than thirty million copies have been printed worldwide.

Decades later, Margaret Mitchell again displayed her non-conformist side when the Atlanta Junior League hosted the jubilant citywide premiere party for the film. Everyone who was anyone associated with the film would be there: Gable, Howard, Leigh, de Haviland, Selznick, and their just as popular dates or spouses. Stubborn, gutsy, and defiant, she declined their invitation.

Now in its 80th year of distribution, *Gone with the Wind,* is the winner of ten Academy Awards.

I feel sure with both behaviors, Margaret Mitchell was thinking, "I'll show you!"

(Lesson Three in 'Intolerance')

Here's another story that caught my attention.

Jay Gatz is a fictional character from F. Scott Fitzgerald's *The Great Gatsby.* In 1917 as a young military officer, he meets Daisy Buchanan in Louisville before leaving to fight in World War I. Although not Daisy's class of people, she can't seem to forget him. The movie of the same name, Jay Gatz is played by Robert Redford. I get it.

Daisy, her family, and friends are an elitist group. As the story progresses, they represent not so much on how much money one has, but where that money came from and when it was acquired. Gatz coming from humble beginnings knows to win Daisy over he must become rich. He changes his name to Gatsby and becomes a self-made man, admirable, but Gatsby's money did not come from inheritance, as he would like people to believe. His money comes from organized crime.

For "old money" people, Gatsby's newly acquired money is reason enough to dislike him. Their way of thinking is Gatsby cannot possibly have the same refinement, sensibility, and taste they themselves have: he works for a living, coming from a low-class background which means he cannot possibly be like them, in their opinion.

With his newfound fortune and not having a firm grasp on reality, he thinks he can turn back time and start over as a wealthy man who can woo Daisy away from her now husband, Tom, and their child. Her life has changed with a marriage and child, yet Gatsby still sees her perfection as he did in Louisville and wants to recapture those moments. But this is something no man, no matter how rich or charming, can do.

The moral of *The Great Gatsby* is that the American Dream is ultimately unattainable for Gatsby even with his great wealth and status as a socialite. He'll never be like Daisy and Tom Buchanan.

Fitzgerald sets up his novel into distinct social classes but in the end, each has its own problems to deal with. He sends strong messages about the elitism running throughout every strata of society – old money, new money, and no money. The "old money" people like Daisy and Tom, were born into wealth having had money for generations and portrayed as people who do not have to work while amusing themselves with whatever takes their fancy.

The narrator, Nick Carroway, Daisy's cousin, is from Minnesota and has moved to New York to work on Wall Street. As her cousin, he is respectable but also has a respectable position in stocks and bonds. Whereas Tom's mistress, Myrtle, wife of Tom's mechanic, has no money and is easily persuaded to leave her drab life for a few hours of glee with Tom. Myrtle is no more than a toy to Tom and those he represents.

In many ways, Fitzgerald claims the social elite are right: the "new money" people cannot be like them. They aren't nice people, are judgmental, and superficial. They fail to look at the essence of the people around them and themselves. They live their lives to perpetuate their sense of superiority however unrealistic.

Fitzgerald's novel is commended for its social commentary. I think Joseph Kennedy's life parallels this story from the previous decade, but Margaret Mitchell's does not. Agree?

Speedy Gonzales

Just when I thought I might be losing my funny bone because of my self-induced isolation and not getting out much to seek or cause chaos, I left my home with my secure homemade mask (made of staples, rubber bands, and recommended canvas cloth, which I will gladly make for you for $.99), to get my car tag registered for this year. Outside, the courthouse was lined with people for the same reason. I was told I had a twenty-minute wait.

Watching people walk up a ramp and in another door labeled VOTING, I figured I had time to vote. One of the outside helpers managing the lines overheard me say to Hubby that, while at the courthouse, I could probably vote, too, and encouraged me with my wait time to go ahead. I did.

Showing my driver's license identification verifying my likeness and proof of residence, I walked right in. Once inside, I again submitted all my proof of identify and was given my little green card to insert into the voting machine.

There were three machines operating instead of the normal six to provide the six feet of separation between voters. Inserting the card, I began voting. Easy peasy and I still had fourteen minutes before walking into the tag office.

I hadn't experienced the printout ballot before. Is this new? Was it implemented because of possible voter fraud? Did it verify the voter with a printout? The printer whirred as I watched the piece of paper scroll out. When it was about three-fourths done, I started to manually pull the piece of paper out when it would not let me and rolled backwards into the machine. And there it stuck.

You know the joke, "How many people does it take to retrieve a piece of paper from a printer?" The answer? Three. Well, maybe four. There was a supervisor supervising. One assessed the situation. Another came with a key to unlock something or other on the printer. The last one was like an IT guy except he was knowledgeable about printers. However, he had to decipher another unused printer to make sure he was solving this problem correctly. It was a mess.

But after a while of watching one poll manager after another trying to retrieve the paper out of the machine because I *had* to have that paper identifying my vote before I left that room, it became comical to me. Not to them, mind you. I still had five minutes until I was allowed into the inner sanctum of the courthouse to stand in line again for the tag office.

Trying to find the humor in the situation like Erma Bombeck would when she was quoted as saying, "It you can't make it better, laugh at it," I repeated these words. They did not think it was funny. I heard one of the three involved mutter "Why me?" I then commented again about my mistake of pulling the paper ballot out of the machine too fast and said, "Surely someone else has done this before?" Nope. Well, in my opinion at least now they would have practice for future quick responders like me…but did they thank me?

Finally, as the problem was getting corrected with three minutes before they were going to allow me to enter the tag office I said, "Well, at least should you see me on the street, you can't identify me as the culprit because I am wearing a mask."

Eventually, all three retreated back inside another office from whence they came, and the printer scrolled out the paper I was supposed to have before leaving. And guess what I had to do with it once it was in my hands? *Throw it in a shredder*!

But there is a silver lining: I made it to the tag office on time where they had to take my temperature before entering and so now I know *all is well*.

The Little Blue Book No. 987

I am not a person who saves unnecessary objects or hoards things. While purging stuff in my closet, I came across a little book which I had seen before but never opened. It has moved from house to house with us with no place to really land…not the office, not a guest bedroom drawer, not even my library (which is its next stop) but somehow made its way into *my* closet. It isn't mine. It belongs to the ~~pack rat~~ collector in my home and I think his mother gave it to him.

It is only 64 pages with three of those for other titles by the same publisher. The book's title: *The Art of Kissing*. Edited and published by E. Haldeman-Julius.

Emanuel Haldeman-Julius was born July 30, 1889 and died July 31, 1951. He was a Jewish-American socialist writer, an atheist thinker, social reformer, and publisher. He is best remembered for creating a series of pamphlets known as "Little Blue Books". Sales totaled into the hundreds of millions of copies.

Born in Philadelphia, Pennsylvania, he was the son of David Julius, a bookbinder. His parents fled Odessa (then part of the Russian Empire) and emigrated to America to escape religious persecution. Both his paternal and maternal grandfathers had been rabbis, but his own parents were indifferent to the Jewish faith.

As a boy, Emanuel read voraciously. Literature and pamphlets produced by the socialists were inexpensive; Julius read them and was convinced by their arguments. He joined the Socialist Party before World War I and was the party's Senatorial candidate for the state of Kansas in 1932.

Working for various newspapers, Julius rose to particular prominence as an editor with the socialist newspaper, *Appeal to Reason*. It had a large national circulation but was on the decline. When he married his first wife, Marcet Haldeman (whose last name he adopted in hyphenation), he purchased the *Appeal to Reason*'s printing operation in Girard, Kansas and began printing the 3.5" X 5" pocketbooks on cheap pulp paper (similar to that used in pulp magazines), stapled in paper cover. The covers were either yellow or red.

They were first called *The Appeal's Pocket Series* and sold for 25 cents in 1919. After several name changes, they finally settled on *Little Blue Books* in 1923. The five-cent price of the books remained for many years. Many titles of classic literature were changed becoming lurid in order to increase sales. For instance, in the passion series, *Don Juan: A Passion in the Desert*; *Sarah Bernhardt's Philosophy of Love*; *The King Enjoys Himself* (a Victor Hugo drama re-titled); *The Happy Hypocrite*; *Illicit Love and Other Tales*; *Casanova and the Women He Loved*; *A Wife's Confession and Other Stories*, and more.

No wonder millions of copies per year were sold in the late 1920s.

The Art of Kissing, published in 1926, contains the following chapter contents:

Chapter 1 – The Origin of Kissing, Defining a Kiss, Roots of Kissing, The Two Kinds of Kissing.

Chapter 2 – The History of Lip Kissing, In Antiquity, The Spread of Kissing.

Chapter 3 – The Techniques of the Kiss, The First Kiss, The Sophisticated Kiss, a Girl's Kiss.

Chapter 4 – Special Problems, Size of a Mouth, Kissing Relatives, Kissing Your Own Sex, The Kiss Complete.

Chapter 5 – Kissing Customs, The Religious Kiss, On Special Occasions, Kissing Games and Sports, Kissing Devices.

Chapter 6 – Celebrated Kisses, Kissing the Blarney Stone, The Poets on Kissing, The Octopus Kiss, The Kiss of Death, The Kiss and Love.

In any case, probably more than you need or want to know about kissing.

Do you remember your first kiss? I was in the fourth grade and finally got up the nerve to kiss Richard Mays, a sixth grader while several of us were in the neighborhood playing outside. With a quick peck on his cheek, I turned and ran away hoping to never have to see him again. That didn't happen. Luckily, he never mentioned it. And I didn't land an octopus kiss – whatever that is - on him, I don't think. But I imagine he was embarrassed all the same.

Fractured Fairytale: Snow White

I received a phone call the other day. I am always receiving phone calls from my fairy tale friends. These make-believe characters are unbelievable. That is a rhetorical statement, ya' know?

The situations they get themselves into! Their lives, on paper (as in a book, get it?), are so seemingly perfect. Then just when you think that things are going to be "happily ever after" – like marrying a prince or something – you turn the page, and they aren't content after all. Maybe there should be something written at the end of their stories like, "…and the moral of the story is…" so that they will have a heads up about their fate. Maybe then they will learn to think before they act. But they don't learn. They just act or react with no thought of the consequences. As quickly as you can say, "Bibbidy, Bobbidy, Boo!" they don't stop and think about the long-term ramifications of their immediate actions.

Who really knows what goes on in other people's castles? But it can't all be perfect like in the story books because when Snow White recently called me, she was unhappy with her "Happy Ending" and needed to vent.

(phone rings)

LSJ: Hello? Oh, hello Snow White. No, this is a good time. What's up?

(listening)

LSJ: Why are you bitter? You say you've grown old and need to live up to the fairy tale standards of looking youthful like in the beginning of your story?

(listening)

LSJ: I know you are not a princess anymore. You are a QUEEN! Think about it. How wonderful to have the wisdom, experience, and influence that age gives you. Not to mention jewels, crowns, prom dresses, and such. (Pause) Yes, I know princesses are girlish and queens are old. You can't expect to be the fairest forever.

(listening)

LSJ: You are thinking about what? Having some work done to help you look fresh again? What kind of work? Won't it be noticeable?

(listening)

LSJ: No, it's not Mirror, Mirror's fault. Everyone would want to look naturally young forever and yes, it's an impossible fairy tale to live up to.

(listening)

LSJ: Snow, at least you aren't vain like the last queen. Didn't Mirror, Mirror say it was exhausting to hear her ask every minute of every day, "Who's the fairest? Who's the fairest?" All she wanted was validation. At least you are seeing yourself for what you are.

(listening)

LSJ: I get it. One day you are the darling of the woods and living with 7 men in a cottage who adored you. They hung on to every word you spoke, and they catered to your every whim. Then next thing you know, you are what you are: old and no one listens to you. They dismiss that you could know anything at all. Ageism! I mean, you are older than me and I don't even like it!

(listening)

LSJ: Oh, I am sorry. Did I hurt your feelings? Well, let's get real, Snow. You were in your late teens in 1937 for your debut. I mean, it's just the circle of life.

(listening)

LSJ: But I understand about having that adoration when you were young. You were definitely one of Disney's "IT" girls.

(listening)

LSJ: Well, Snow, think long and hard before you decide on plastic surgery. No, you haven't become desexualized into a matron like Fairy Godmother…yet. But it won't be long now. Remember, you are over 100. At least you still have a good personality and while in the cottage in the woods, you learned how to make all your own clothes and bake apple pies.

And with that, she hung up.

This Little Piggy

With summer's end, I probably need to get a new toenail polish color. When I find something I like, I tend to stick with it. This summer I was loving on this raspberry color that I'd been wearing. I don't have to keep up with the name at all. I just leave it up to the professional giving me the pedicure. I walk into the salon and they ask me to pick a color. I have an appointment with the same gal every time, she knows my likes, so I just point out what's on my toes from the previous visit and she either has it in her little suitcase or she knows where on the wall to retrieve it with all the other paint colors.

I do the same with my makeup. It's all Lancôme. I don't keep up with the names on the makeup that I purchase for eyes, or base for my face, or blush for my cheeks, etc. I just bring in the almost empty bottle or mascara wand, hand them to the counter's clerk, tell her I want more of the same, and VOILA!

That may sound crazy not to know the names or colors of the makeup I purchase but that kind of fluff information clogs my brain. I need to not have it any more congested than it already is. Why try to remember something when I know I won't eventually be able to anyway. I can't remember stuff I am *supposed* to be able to now. That's depressing enough.

But while reading a female oriented fashion magazine, I found an interesting article about the new and hip fingernail polishes. I only use clear on my fingernails. I leave the color to the toes so they can peep out color from various sandals I wear in the summer and really even early Fall because as we all know, it's still damn hot in Atlanta. You know what we're

113

called: Hotlanta. And it's just like that in the summer. I can remember some Christmases in the high 70s. So, I'll still be wearing certain types of open toed shoes.

But now that it is turning to Autumn, shouldn't I exchange my Raspberry-something-or-other to a more acceptable Fall hue? Sure, Cinnamon and Spice come to mind in the Fall when you think of homemade apple pies, Pilgrims, and the changing leaf colors on the trees. So, I couldn't resist. Here are a few I am considering:

Putrefied Plum, Tainted Tan, Burnt Buffalo Brown, Contaminated Copper, Gross Gold, Foul Fowl, Rank Red, Whiffy Weimaraner Grey, Malodorous Maroon, Decomposed Chestnuts, Stale Squishy Squash, Nidorous Nuts, Dam! Beavers, Tainted Tumbleweed, Moldy Mauve, Nauseating Navy, Obnoxious Orchid, Disgusting Denim Blue, Old Olive, Revolting Red, Funky Forest Green, Mephitic Mountain Meadow, Fetid Fern, Smelly Sneakers, Rancid Robins Egg Blue, Blah Blush, Disgusting Dried Dandelions, Pungent Pumpkins, and Gamy Granny Smith Apples.

Pick your favorite and ask your nail technician to hold it for you so you, too, can be hip this Fall with the newest nail color.

Notable KD Ladies

Sorority recruitment has just ended for many universities. Being a sorority sister means hard work maintaining the expected grade point average, attending chapter meetings, taking on leadership roles, and working on your chapter's philanthropy.

Here are a few notable women who have a KD Lady attached to their names. I am proud to call them my Kappa Delta sisters.

1. Pearl S. Buck - one of the most famous writers of her time and won Pulitzer Prize in 1932 for her bestselling novel' The Good Earth'. Pearl S. Buck was awarded Nobel Prize in Literature in 1938.
2. Georgia O'Keefe - She is one of the most famous American artists and recipient of the highest national honor 'The Medal of Freedom' awarded to her by President Gerald R. Ford.
3. Joan Lowery Nixon – was a famous author specializing in fiction and mystery for children and young adults. She had written more than one hundred books and is four times winner of the Edgar Allan Poe Awards.
4. Bonnie Jeanne Dunbar - Dunbar has spent more than 1208 hours (50 days) in Space. She is one of the most experienced female astronauts in the world. Her space missions include STS-89, STS-50, STS-71, STS-32, and STS-61. She won five Space Flight Medals. Dunbar was inducted into the Women in

Technology International (WITI) Hall of fame. She is one of only five in the world holding this honor.

5. Claudia Kennedy - now retired, she is the first female to reach the rank of three-star general in the US Army.

6. Kathleen Babineau Blanco - She was the 78th Governor of Louisiana and the first female elected for this position.

7. Margret Holland Sargent - She was one of the most famous Portrait artists, based in Los Angeles. She has painted more than 300 oil portraits including portraits of Tennessee Williams, Gerald Ford, Jimmy Carter, and Margret Thatcher.

8. Trischa Zorn – Blind by birth, Trischa is a champion swimmer. She has won 55 medals in Paralympic games, more won than by any other athlete in that category in the world. Out of the 55 medals, 41 are gold medals.

9. Debbie Maffett Wilson – crowned Miss California, she won the Miss America title in 1983.

10. Ali Landry – now a television personality, she won Miss USA in 1996.

11. Brooke Anderson – an Emmy and Peabody award-winning TV host and journalist.

12. Patricia "Sister" Wood Barnes – turned her Sister Schubert's Homemade Rolls from sharing with family members into a multimillion-dollar corporation.

13. Ruth Johnson Colvin – founder of Literacy Volunteers of American and an inductee of the

National Women's Hall of Fame and earned the Presidential Medal of Freedom.

14. Lynne Martin Doughtie – named Fortune magazine's Most Powerful Women in business.

15. Suzy Spafford Lidstrom – her Suzy's Zoo products won the National Cartoonist Society Greeting Card Award in 1996.

16. Patricia Polito Miller – co-founder of Vera Bradley Designs.

17. Cara Mund - crowned Miss America 2018.

18. Gloria Ray - established the Women's Basketball Hall of Fame. She was the first president of the Southeastern Conference Women's Athletic Directors.

19. Lara Von Seelen Spencer - is a co-anchor for ABC's Good Morning America and host for the Great American County Channel and HGTV's Flea Market Flip.

20. Janet Marie Smith - renowned architect and urban planner. She oversaw upgrades to Dodger Stadium, Oriole Park at Camden Yards, Fenway Park and Turner Field. Her preservation of historic Fenway Park placed the ballpark on the National Historic Register.

21. Leigh Anne Tuohy and her husband, Sean, who adopted Michael Oher, an at-risk teenager, encouraged him to fulfill his dream of becoming a professional football player. Their story was the basis of the book and blockbuster film, *The Blind Side*.

This is just a sample of the Kappa Deltas that honor our creed, 'Let us strive for that which is honorable, beautiful, and highest.'

I'll Give You a Minute
to Mullet it Over

Hey, y'all.

Do you remember the 1980s and the mullet haircut? You may have worn one yourself. Don't feel embarrassed. Well, maybe you should if someone pulls out some old-timey picture of you with one. Don't feel bad. You were in good company - George Clooney, Brad Pitt, Paul McCartney, Jerry Seinfeld, Michael Bolton, and many more had that same hairdo. Today Billy Ray Cyrus and Rod Stewart still keep theirs.

Say what? Some of you do not know what the mullet is. There is even a book, *The Mullet: Hairstyle of the Gods* by Mark Larson for you to read and reminisce about your previous haircut…or educate some of you if you have not been exposed to that 'do' of the 1980s. If you are not aware what a mullet hairstyle is, the mullet-cut is a style in which the hair is short at the front coupled with a long mane in the back. Let's be real – it's really just a neck beard! The mullet has been making people ugly since the dawn of time. Think of the Geico Caveman commercial. I'll give you a minute to *mullet* it over.

Also think about Samson and his story from the Bible. Samson's long hair served a purpose and if it was ever cut, he would lose his strength. Many of the Biblical movies from the 20th century had the men of the Bible wear the mullets.

There are some celebrities who continue to own one: Billy Ray Cyrus and Rod Stewart come to mind. And do you wonder why they keep the same haircut? My guess is they know the secret of never looking old in pictures. Can anyone say with certainty, "Is that picture of Billy Ray from the 1980s or 2000s?" or "That Rod Stewart never seems to age." Well, that's because he has *always* looked old. You really can't tell. And that's the point. Keep the same do and you never grow old in pictures.

The celebrities that moved on did so sooner than later but then there was Michael Bolton! He kept his style a little too long. Man his was ugly as homemade sin. I don't know why there is the saying, "Business up front. Party in the back." But I do believe that it's true to say the mullet blocks the sun, therefore you can't get a red neck.

Did President Trump have a partial mullet in the 1980s? I know his was long in front, but it was longer in back. But wasn't most everyone you knew in that decade carrying this cut? He was no different trying to be stylish, but whoever told him that hairdo looked good, lied. Not even Chuck Norris or Joe Dirt can pull this 'do' off.

Women were just as bad: Ellen DeGeneres, had one. **Florence Henderson just about beats all of the women who ever had a mullet.** You know her…the mom from the 1970s Brady Bunch TV show? Bless their hearts.

I think if you keep the same style cut you never look old. Think back on Doris Day, Princess Grace, and Audrey Hepburn. Today those still looking young with the same cut are: Halle Berry, Julianne Moore, Sandra Bullock, and Jennifer Aniston.

And maybe Donald Trump.

In the Summer of '65

Have you heard about *Yesterday,* the 2019 British jukebox musical and romantic comedy? A struggling musician, who after an accident, finds himself the only person who remembers the Beatles. Can you imagine? He becomes famous taking credit for writing and performing their songs. Reminds me a little about *Back to the Future*'s Marty McFly's nemesis, Biff, who comes across a sports almanac containing decades of winning teams and their scores and while living in the past, bets on the future winning teams, makes a fortune, and runs and ruins Hill Valley.

The filmmakers had to get the rights to include the Beatles' music. Ten million dollars later, they did and although none of the band was involved, producers received blessings from the Beatles and their families.

On August 18, 1965, the Beatles made their only Georgia appearance and I saw them perform. I would say I heard them, but that was impossible because of the 30,000 screaming voices at Atlanta Fulton County Stadium. They were in town less than ten hours and although they never landed in Georgia again, Beatlemania was alive and well in Atlanta. The *Atlanta Journal* had a story about how to give a Beatle haircut. Mayor Ivan Allen, in a pre-concert press conference, gave the Beatles the key to the city. The Beatles were gracious enough to be quoted as saying Georgians Otis Redding and James Brown were on their list of favorite musicians.

And there I was, twelve years old at my first concert, seeing the Beatles…*with my parents*. The only way they would let me attend is if they went with me. With parents forty years older than me, do you know how embarrassing it was to sit there next to two 52-year-olds? And waiting along side them while at least six warm-up acts played to arouse the crowd was awful to endure.

But finally, at 9:37 p.m., the mop-heads from Liverpool ran out of the third-base dugout as the stadium erupted in screams while flashbulbs popped, and girls fainted. They began their set with "Twist and Shout", played eleven more songs, then disappeared into a limo behind the concert stage, and raced to the airport.

My thirteen-year-old female cousin and three of her friends of the same age were allowed to attend without parental supervision. Her parents dropped the four girls off and picked them back up later for the half-hour ride back to the suburbs. I bet she had a better time than I did. She probably screamed as loud as she wanted (… so loud she might have even lost her voice); stand up in her seat, act like a fool, and pretend she was about to faint; and, heck, maybe she even cried. There would be no one there to stop her. But over at the geriatric seats, I had to be calmer and more collected, so I didn't contribute to bursting my parents' ear drums. It was frustrating to say the least. I wanted to act young because I was young, yet…there were these old people sitting next to me.

I guess it might have been worse for my hometown next-door-neighbor-friends and *their* parents. Living within twenty-five miles of the stadium, we all rode up together and sat next to each other at the concert. There I was with my friends, who were really like sisters to me, and their parents who would eventually become our neighbors for fifty years.

Them and us. Together. At least I was twelve. How really embarrassing for these girls whose parents didn't let them go off by themselves at the ages of fifteen and eighteen.

I am sure we were a queer sight.

P.S. After fifty-four years, I still have my concert program and the three tickets that my family purchased. They are framed and are in a prominent place at our lake home as a conversation starter and retelling this Beatles concert story. When people play the game on Facebook about, "What was the first concert you attended?" Look what I get to say.

I Could Care Less?

James R. Fitzgerald, acting unit chief in the FBI's Behavioral Analysis Unit-1, had been with the agency for almost twenty years when one of his biggest cases came to an end all because of semantics. All the cunning in the world for entrapment came down to the way a killer formed his words in his writing.

Know who I am talking about? Ted Kaczynski, the Unabomber.

Fitzgerald recalled how a transposition of verbs in Kaczynski's manifesto led to a closer identification in April 1996. He used the phrase "You can't eat your cake and have it, too," instead of the usual phrase, "You can't have your cake and eat it, too." Fitzgerald, like most people, thought he had made a mistake. But examinations of other letters by Kaczynski contained a similar feature, which, Mr. Fitzgerald said, "is actually a traditionally middle English way of using the term. He technically had it right and the rest of us had it wrong. It was one of the big clues that allowed us to make the rest of the comparison and submit a report to the judge who signed off on a search warrant."

I mean, think about it. The phrase should be the way the Unabomber wrote it. It just doesn't make sense the other way around. Why, of course, one can have their cake and eat it. Isn't that how it's done? (Unless someone is stopping you, of course.) But one can't eat their cake and still make it available. See?

What other phrases are we saying incorrectly? Here are some of the most commonly misused phrases that might have slipped under your radar.

Let's begin with the #1 most irritating one in *my* mind.

1. I Could Care Less. I wish I could say that <u>I couldn't care less</u> when you say this phrase, but golly! Saying it this way drives me crazy. If you could care less, then you *could care less*.

2. Hunger pains. That growling is your stomach telling you that it's bored, not hungry and it is pronounced <u>hunger pangs</u>.

3. Escape goat. You've got to be *kidding* me. Only use this when your goat has escaped your yard. All other times it refers to someone who's being blamed for another's wrongdoings and is called a <u>scapegoat</u>. Remember, it's not the mistake *you* make that's important. It's how you *shift the blame*.

4. Ex-patriot. Tina Turner temporarily used to be one when she first moved to Switzerland to save money on her taxes. Now she is an <u>expatriate</u> because she has been there for decades and no longer has any ties to the U.S.

5. Pass Mustard. Need some for your burger or hot dog? I *relish* the idea to clear this up for you. If something <u>passes muster</u>, it means that something is satisfactory.

6. Biting my time. What are you biting to pass the time? Your nails? You should be <u>biding your time</u> by doing something more constructive, maybe. Remember it this way: What was the current President of the United States doing before his inauguration? He was BIDEN his time.

7. Piece of Mind. I have a friend who deals with his <u>peace of mind</u> this way. "One day I was born. Then everything bothered me. And that brings us up to date." He's at peace with this explanation about how he handles life.

8. First-Come, First-Serve. The last thing you'd ever want to hear is "first-come, first-serve." Trust me. Written this way implies that the first person who arrives at a restaurant or party is also the one who has to serve all the other guests. To avoid this, say "<u>first-come, first-served</u>."

9. Make Due. The only person who can make due is the person who has given an assignment or deadline for a project. The rest of the time is <u>making do</u>. I am making do with this: "All due respect" is a wonderful expression because it doesn't actually specify how much respect is actually due. Could be none.

So I have discussed "I could care less." Now let's move on to "I could of…"

Of? Could *of*? Could, should, and would are auxiliary verbs that can be defined as past tenses of will, shall, and can, which helps a verb. Verbs are words used to describe an action, state, or occurrence. If I was still teaching, this is how I would make the point that *of* is not a verb… "If you can stand up and *of* then it's a verb. Everyone stand up and *of*." (Not happening.)

One should be saying, "…could have…" So, obviously using *of* with could, should, or would irks me. Notice I used an Oxford comma in that last sentence. Don't get me started on the Oxford comma.

Now, back to our list.

10. One in the same – The correct phrase is *one and the same* if what you are trying to say is that two things are indistinguishable. Think of this when trying to get it right: "I'm not insulting you. I am describing you."

11. Nip It in the Butt – The image you may conjure up here is the ad with the Coppertone girl at the beach and the cute puppy playfully biting at her posterior. The correct phrase, *nip it in the bud*, should be used when talking about halting something in process, like in plants. Yes, nipping it in the bud should now be an image of trimming a flower at an early age so it can't grow or Barney Fife constantly saying, "Nip It!"

12. Butt naked – how appropriate it should follow Nip It in the Butt. The saying is actually *buck naked* and it refers to a man's buttocks being exposed, but (pun intended), Amazon can solve that problem with their advertisement of the Duluth Trading Company Men's Buck Naked Performance Boxers. Prices begin at $28.99. The ad says it has 4 used and new boxers.

13. You've Got Another Thing Coming- or if you are from the South, you might hear a Southern Mama say, "If you think for one second I am going to put up with that, y'all got another thang comin'.'" Although it makes some sense in that you assume one thing, but it will turn out to be incorrect (like this saying) because said accurately, it's *you've got*

127

another think coming. This means another thought or belief will soon replace the one you currently hold true.

14. Do a 360 - Traveling 360 degrees leaves you right where you started but traveling 180 degrees leaves you as far from your starting point as possible. *Do a 180* is the correct phrase. Be smart about it because when your instructions for a premade pie asks you to put it in the oven at 180 degrees, don't put it in upside down.

15. Honing In - I understand why this one might confuse you because honing seems correct as it means to sharpen a skill. But use *homing in*. Ever heard of a homing missile? "To home" means "to get closer to," either figuratively or literally. To remember homing, you can make lots of money selling homing pigeons on eBay.

16. Worse Comes to Worse - According to the *New York Times*, the statement, "worst come to the worst" was first published in 1596 meaning a hypothetical worst-case scenario turning into a real-life worst-case scenario. It is more commonly known today as *worse comes to worst* indicating the possibility of a bad situation becoming a terrible one. Again, if you are from the South, it might be said this way, "She went from the frying pan into the fire."

If you want more of these, let me know. ~Lee

WART Are You Talking About?

Sometime around 1961 when I was about eight years old, my mother noticed a wart between two of my fingers on my left hand. It might have been unsightly, but to me it was uncomfortable. Warts are caused by a virus. It is said that most will go away, after a time, by themselves. But who knows when?

One summer day, she drove down a country road in my Georgia hometown taking me to what I now know is called a 'traiteur'. *Traiteurs*, or "treaters" in English, are the traditional folk medicine healers of south Louisiana. Cajuns, Creoles, and Native Americans all participate in this Catholic healing ritual. There are many types of *traiteurs*; some use herbal remedies (*remèdes*), gestures such as the sign of the Cross or the laying on of hands, or material objects such as knotted string, a cordon, which is tied around the affected area, in their treatments, but all of them use prayer. Faith in God's power to heal is the heart of this practice. *Traiteurs* can treat a wide variety of ailments, including but by no means limited to warts, such as sunstroke, bleeding, arthritis, and asthma, however their services are not for sale. Patients tend to reciprocate by offering a gift of appreciation, but not even the empty-handed will ever be refused treatment. The gift of treating is usually passed from an older traiteur to a younger person, often in the same family.

This woman rubbed on my wart and talked what seemed like mumbo-jumbo directly to it. I do not remember what my mother gave to thank her. I've read that when rubbed by another person or if the 'traiteur' licks their own fingers and

129

then rubs it on the other person's wart, the chemical reaction from their DNA sometimes speeds up the process of having a wart fall off. And this is exactly what happened. Although there was no licking involved, within two weeks, it was gone.

Sometimes it is a little more involved. Not only touching the wart but sometimes the person commencing the wart ceremony will do some kind of speaking, as in my case, and the wart disappears. But, other 'traiteurs' have their own remedies for warts. Some involve potatoes. It seems if you cut a potato in half and rub it on the wart, and then bury that tater, it would remove your wart. I've also heard of using a fat piece of meat and burying it afterwards.

Of course, there's muriatic acid if you don't want to take these routes. But that sure ain't fun. Or as a couple of others expressed, "My brother, just a year older, and I used to fight all the time. He 'conjured' a wart off my nose – with a right hook one day. Never came back!"

But my personal favorite is, "I had an uncle who would bite them off. Of course, he was from the old country and would eat anything."

Bubble Girl

I think I am depressed. With all the stuff going on in life – from COVID to the behaviors in the election, I've decided to hide in a bubble. No kidding, I am creating my own fantasy environment and I am starting by watching as many Hallmark Christmas movies as possible that I can.

As of February 2015, Hallmark Channel is available to approximately 73.4% of U.S. households with a television. What have I been missing? Always thinking they were cheesy while everyone else was going gaga over their movies, I finally succumbed. I need some uplifting in today's conditions: fake snow, a Santa, and Christmas decorating should do it.

I recently watched A SNOWCONE CHRISTMAS. Have you seen it? Here is the plot summary: Marty McColeman operates the coolest (pun intended) snow cone kiosk in St. Claire, Michigan. He is a second-generation snow cone operator. He and his dad work the stand six months out of the year, and you'd think it would be the summer months, but NO!

His father is deaf in one ear so only hears half of what is being said, but he is a pretty good lip reader. In the first thirty minutes, we see the town people interacting with the McColemans who they have known for decades and have come to know and love.

Commercial Break: It's for Nair Shaving Cream. I don't understand having this commercial about shaving one's legs when the women in Michigan rarely show their legs. They either have leggings, boots, slacks, or muumuus. Oh, well.

Back to the storyline. Marty is about fifty years old. His dad is around seventy-five and they live together. These two men have one of the most impeccably decorated houses in town. I can't believe why two old men go all out to decorate like that. Beside their own home, we see the entire town is festive when the McColemans sell their cones to various visitors and merchants. We get a glimpse of the town square, its ginormous Christmas tree with colored lights, and the local bakery where everyone visits all the time, yet no one gets fat while ordering their muffins, cookies, and hot cocoa. They drink a lot of hot cocoa. It's never, "Would you like to go and get a drink?" It's "Would you like to go and get a cocoa?" Maybe they are pouring other stuff in the cocoa. I'd like that recipe.

Commercial: This time it is for another Hallmark movie coming soon called, CHRISTMAS PUPPY. You know that one is going to be a tearjerker. It also has tons of decorations, lots of snow, pretty people with pretty white teeth, white lights, cocoa, and a dog. Betty White stars.

When our story continues, Marty is competing for the distinguished title "Snow Cone of the Year", which, since he is the only person who sells snow cones, he has won an unprecedented 20 times since the contest first started *by his dad*.

But before he does, there has to be conflict. Marty has lost this year's new recipe…a most unusual flavor for his 21st try – Fruitcake Snow Cone. It was going to be a difficult flavor and he is now in trouble because he is not able to find it.

Commercial: Betty Crocker and the company is pushing their fruitcake cake mix. Someone is doing a good job of researching advertising sponsors.

Bucky, Marty's Jack Russell Terrier (there has to be a dog) saves the day. He finds the valuable recipe in the trash (dogs always get in the trash) and returns it to his owner. This part was a little tricky and hard to believe. However, "All's well that ends well" because Marty wins again.

Cast: Bucky – played by Eddie from TV's "Frasier".

Marty McColeman – Henry Winkler

Mr. McColeman - Dabney Coleman (what a coincidence!)

Even though it's getting colder, this movie makes me want a snow cone.

I give it 2 stars because it has a dog and cocoa.

Coming up: a review for SANTA SAID "YOU BETTER NOT CRY OR I'LL GIVE YOU SOMETHING TO CRY ABOUT."

Glue Stick's Last Christmas

Having started watching Hallmark Christmas Movies to chase off the blues from COVID and the chaos from the recent Presidential election, I found that reviewing these movies has helped my mental health tremendously. Maybe you should consider escaping into pretend-land with a few movies, too.

I recently became absorbed with Hallmark's latest – "Glue Sticks Last Christmas". Yes, it's about a horse farm in Sheffield, Kentucky. Don't give up on the title yet…you know Hallmark likes to pull the strings of your heart and then have a happy ending. This one does not disappoint.

If you have been thinking the repairman in the Maytag commercials is a hunk, you'll be happy to know he is our protagonist. Boy, he does clean up well when he isn't in his Maytag uniform. Youza! Clark Redmond possesses a horse farm and rents stables to the horses' owners. He also grows and sells Christmas trees to neighbors and their friends.

Christmas is around the corner and Clark is hosting an Open House on his property and selling his trees. His home's porch is decorated with one of his trees he cut from his tree farm and stands about twelve feet tall. Since Clark lives alone, I don't know who in the hell helped him decorate that tree to perfection since it stands high with large silver balls, real red cranberry garlands, a multitude of white lights, and fake snowflake ornaments adorning the tree to match the fake snow on the ground.

A crowd starts to gather in line to enjoy his homemade apple Wassail for the adults, hot cocoa for the children, and gingerbread cookies for all, when it is time to cut to a commercial.

This commercial is for Nestle's Hot Chocolate. What an appropriate moment to break away from this winter movie with a nice hot cup of cocoa. Personally, I'd rather have a commercial on how to make homemade Wassail using Kentucky's Jim Beam whiskey.

The story continues with Clark allowing a pony ride for the children on Glue Stick, a really old mild-mannered horse who has seen better days and is going out for his last round of pony rides. Clark has been taking care of the horse since the horse's owner moved to a large city in another state. Poor thing! The horse loves the children and the children love him and know he is on his last legs (idiom intended). It just costs too much to keep up an old horse. But the children come up with a plan.

Commercial for Elmer's Glue Sticks. Was this really necessary? I had to leave during this commercial. I was starting to cry.

When I return, the children know they have to do something to save the day. They decide to hold an ugly horse contest and have the county folks in the area (in Kentucky, everyone loves horses) pay to vote on the ugliest horse at Clark's stables. The children's parents, who by now started drinking the Wassail with Jim Beam (one of the dads clandestinely brought along enough whiskey to pour in their beverages) start to think the children's idea is GENUIS!

Commercial: You've guessed it. It's a Maytag commercial with our leading man from the Hallmark story.

Next week at the stables, the children dress up the animals and take pictures, put the horses' pictures on flyers, and staple the flyers to wood light poles in town. But no matter how ugly they try to make the horses look, not one is uglier than the horse they are trying to save. Sponsors' and patrons' money start to flow in.

And they save the day. Enough money has been collected to take care of Glue Stick in his old age. The whole town of Sheffield celebrates at Clark Redmond's with more Wassail, cocoa, and gingerbread cookies.

Cast of characters: Clark Redmond – the Maytag Repairman; Various Children – they all look like the children from the OUR GANG television series.

I give it a 7/10 review because a horse is saved, there is cocoa, and there is Jim Beam whiskey, but there is no dog.

No Hope at Christmas

Having started watching Hallmark Christmas Movies to chase off the blues from COVID and the chaos from the recent Presidential election, I found that reviewing these movies has helped my mental health tremendously. How are you doing?

After seven grandsons, Mel Odious, is tickled pink (idiom intended) learning he now has a granddaughter, Hope. Ira Pent Church in Arkansas was proud to watch Mel's progeny grow up to be a hometown darling.

Like Mel, she has a beautiful singing voice. Hope sang in concerts across the state and although not a beauty, she did win the talent portion in the Miss Arkansas contest. Her claim to fame was winning the State Fair's Hog Calling Contest. No one can "suey" like Hope.

This year's church concert is drawing closer. With so much talent, Mel's granddaughter, Hope Ferdebest, continues being asked to perform with her hometown church choir even though she now lives two hours away. This gifted young lady is the main attraction as she will perform all the solos.

A commercial interrupts this story. I suppose with all the choir members in this movie having pretty white teeth (which we can see during their rehearsals), it would be a natural for Crest to have a commercial.

Returning to our program, we see our soloist clutching at her throat a bit. Have you ever noticed actors asking other actors throughout a program, "Are you OK?" Well, I have and it is so irritating that I started counting. In this show alone, with everyone worried about our soloist, I counted eleven times. (My second most irritating question asked in movies is, "What are you doing here?")

Anyway, she is NOT alright and runs off stage to find a lozenge.

Commercial for? You guessed it. It's Hall's Breezes throat lozenges. These throat drops come in many flavors like strawberry, cherry, raspberry, and grape. I stayed to watch this ad. My throat was beginning to hurt, too.

When we return, there is no sight of our gal! Where could she be? The whole church choir starts looking for her…in the chorus room, in the ladies restrooms, in the dining hall, in the kitchen pantry, in the court yard, in the church library, in the pastor's office, and in the Sunday School classes. I mean everywhere.

She is nowhere to be found, although everyone is wishing and HOPE FERDEBEST.

Then Hallmark holds us in suspense with another commercial; I chose not to watch this one. I changed the channel to watch something to bide my time until the Hallmark movie comes back on. This station's commercial is almost over, so I watch it until the storyline continues.

When it does, there is some man who is sitting in a fast-food restaurant. He eyes a pretty girl sitting in the next booth drinking hot cocoa and rubbing her throat as though she is in pain. She knows this is J.L. Breaker, a convict recently released from jail for stealing chickens from a local farm. The girl becomes nervous and wonders…wait a minute. This is the IDTV channel I changed to during the Hallmark commercial. Let me go back to my movie.

I have now missed how the choir found our soloist, but after they do, the concert practice session can continue (the lozenges she found helped) and now instead of *NO* HOPE AT CHRISTMAS, there <u>will be</u> HOPE AT CHRISTMAS. After the concert there will be punch, popcorn balls, and everyone will gather to build a fake snowman with fake snow.

Cast: Hope Ferdebest – Katy Perry

Mel Odious– Ted Danson

Choir Director – some winner from America's Got Talent – don't know his name

J.L. Breaker – Jack Nicholson

I am giving this movie three out of ten. The church wasn't decorated all that much, no *Hallmark* cocoa, and especially no dog! They asked "Are you OK?" eleven times. I loved the popcorn balls and there was Christmas music sung by a choir, and a frosty snowman, although built with fake snow.

I've been asking myself, "What are you doing here?" so this will be the last Hallmark Christmas movie in 2020 I will watch.

Wishing you and yours a Merry Christmas!

Show-off!

Watching the 2020 Westminster Kennel Club Dog Show I was stunned to find another poodle as the Best in Show. I don't know why. It has wonderful characteristics and they sure do go to enough trouble to make that breed stand out. And he's not even French! Oh? Didn't know it was originally German? POODLE comes from the German *Pudelhund* or *Pude* which in English means "puddle" or "to splash about". The word *Hund* in German means "dog." This dog is a retriever.

The French also used this smart dog as a guide god, guard dog, and military dog. With their coat being moisture-resistant (which helps with swimming) someone thought it was a good idea to help the dogs move through water more efficiently and gave them a cut with patches of hair left on the body to protect the poodle's vital organs and joints from the cold water. Yet they failed to cover their privates.

But why, *why* did they make them look so preposterous? Once they gave them this cut and they looked so dolled-up with their bouffant hair, they started performing at circuses pulling wagons for entertainers. What a low blow from once being a top dog. This dog show is the dog Oscars or the dog Superbowl. These show dogs perform at champion-level and these poor poodles prance around looking like this. Do you think they know?

My family owned several from one breed who made Best in Show three times at Westminster: the Sealyham terrier. It is a Welch breed. I bet you haven't heard of them. They have almost become extinct but are making a comeback. Thank goodness.

Other countries have their designated official dog breed, too. Here is a list of the countries.

Switzerland, Madagascar, Zimbabwe, Norway, Cuba, Republic of Condo, Brazil, and the Netherlands.

Can you match them with the dog breed?

Rhodesian Ridgeback, Fila Brasileiro, Coton de Tulear, St. Bernard, Norwegian Elkhoud, Besenji, Keeshond, and the Havanese.

What about the United States? We, too, have a few states who have their official state dog.

Same game. This time states:

Alaska, Delaware, Louisiana, Maryland, Massachusetts, New Hampshire, North Carolina, Pennsylvania, South Carolina, Tennessee, Texas, Virginia, and Wisconsin.

Match these dog breeds with the states above:

Plott Hound, Blue Tick Coonhound, American Water Spaniel, Catahoula Leopard Dog, Chenook, Boykin Spaniel, American Foxhound, Golden Retriever, Boston Terrier, Great Dane, Blue Lacy, Alaskan Malamute, Chesapeake Bay Retriever.

Here are your answers:

Switzerland – St. Bernard; Madagascar – Coton de Tulear; Zimbabwe – Rhodesian Ridgeback; Norway – Norwegian Elkhound; Cuba – Havanese; Republic of Congo -Besenji; Brazil -Fila Brasileiro; Netherlands – Keeshond

In the states? Alaska - Alaskan Malamute; Delaware – Golden Retriever; Louisiana = Catahoula Leopard dog; Maryland – Chesapeake Bay Retriever; Massachusetts – Boston Terrier; New Hampshire – Chenook; North Carolina – Plott Hound; Pennsylvania – Great Dane; South Carolina – Boykin Spaniel; Tennessee – Blue Tick Coonhound; Texas

– Blue Lacy; Virginia – American Foxhound; and Wisconsin – American Water Spaniel.

Georgia has submitted two entries for a designated state dog – one was the Golden Retriever and most recently – can you guess the other? Here's a hint: Some people call them JUNKYARD DOGS.

What would be your choice?

The Night Before Mutt Day

There are real holidays for dogs. Although, National Mutt Day has passed for this year (December 2nd), I decided to have a little fun with giving it recognition with the poem, "The Night Before Christmas", using the story of Saint Roch.

Saint Roch was born the only child of a wealthy French nobleman around the 14th century. He had a red birthmark in the shape of a cross on his chest. After the deaths of his mother and father at the age of twenty, he renounced his nobility and gave his inheritance to the poor. He eventually contracted the plague and not wanting to infect others, he set off into the forest to die.

While he lay dying, a hunting dog belonging to a count found him and began to care for him. Roch believed the dog was a gift from God. The dog would bring him bread every day and lick his wounds until he made a full recovery. The count, who later discovered what his dog was doing, befriended Roch and let him keep the dog.

'Twas the night before Mutt Day, all through our doghouse,
Snow was on rooftop; we'd nary a douse.
Dog stockings were hung on our roof's eaves with care,
In hopes that Saint Roch soon would be there.

My sisters were nestled all snug in their beds,
while visions of dog biscuits danced in their heads.
Mama in her Auburn collar and I was, too,
Had settled our brains for a dreamy short snooze.

When outside our door there arose such a clatter,
I sprang from my bed to see what was the matter.
The doghouse's front door was open and cold,
Yet, I stood like a sentinel at that threshold.

The moon on the breast of the new-fallen snow
Gave the luster of midday to objects below.
When, what to my wondering eyes did I see?
Saint Roch, saint of all dogs and more baby puppies!

"Now Daschunds! Dalmations! And Goldendoodles!
Terriers! Pugs! and all of you Poodles!
Boxers! And Hounds! All mixed breeds and more!
It's your day to celebrate and your turn to soar!

Saint Roch's story is one to behold,
Since representing all dogs, it's one to enfold.
And pass on to all breeds and all mutts alike,
To tell of his heart and his courage that night.

This might be the story of how dogs became,
Man's best friend or at least some could claim.
A nobleman found himself alone in the woods,
Lost on his journey, hardships he withstood.

While alone in the woods, he soon became ill,
A dog soon appeared with some magical skill.
Because of this dog to whom "I now cherish,
I was taken care of and I did not perish.

This dog saved my life while I was alone
Supplied me with bread, licked wounds that were shown
Which healed me and gave me a brand-new desire,
To look after dogs is what I then aspired."

Born to nobility, tried to help others
He gave away all, to the dogs and their lovers.
So letting you know that "Tomorrow's your day,
National Mutt Day, so go celebrate!"

And with that pronouncement he sped fast away,
We all in amazement were caught in a daze.
Saint Roch had just visited our little home,
We'll not soon forget we've a day of our own.

Surrounded by Idiots

Good Morning Spilling the Beaners! Glad you could join our book club meeting this morning. I am your host, OBie. We meet here on FB every Monday, so always check with us every week and please continue sending in a title you wish us to promote and discuss.

Today's title sent in is called SURROUNDED BY IDIOTS by Thomas Erikson. Are humans the only ones surrounded by idiots? I know a few…

What Mama? That's funny, mama. I'll tell them: Mama wants me to tell you this joke: Did you ever walk into a room and forget why you walked in? That's how dogs spend their lives.

Good one, Mama!

Back to the idiots I know about. While at the dog park I hung out with the owners of the dogs sitting at the picnic table. I overheard a lot! I don't know all these dogs and I may not want to! One mother said her yellow lab dug up the buried hamster in their backyard, then promptly came inside and puked it all up. What an idiot!

One of the dads at the table said while he was browsing the running section in Nike with his dog, Georgia, who took a liking to the AstroTurf grass that was part of the central display and she decided that it would be an appropriate time to take a poop in the middle of the store! He even told the dog's name – which all I have to do is ask the other dogs where Georgia is and keep my distance after hearing this story. I'd never – I am a gentleman.

Another lady said her dog ate an entire rack of cooked pork ribs and got to visit the vet. After three different medicines, her dog never puked. The staff resorted to playing helicopter – spinning around to make him spin around- which they did for 20 minutes to give up the contents of his stomach, which he finally did. However, I also heard his mom say that one of the staff members puked before he did. These guys are idiots!

The conversation went on and on: a pit bull ate half a box of paintballs (around 500) and for the next week he had fluorescent orange poops. An Irish terrier would frequently sneak into a neighbor's garage and steal a can of their dog food stash and come back with it in his mouth hoping we would open it up. Another canine ate her Petco Frisbee in 30 seconds and of course it came out in small red pieces with one still having the Petco name intact.

Oh, of course mama – can't forget this one. Mama's friend has two Australian dogs, JJ and Benny, who love to trick each other. JJ is able to fool his brother into getting up and following him so that JJ can then turn around and take Benny's favorite spot on the dog bed. Now that's a SMART dog.

I've got to try that one with my nephew, Jager sometime.

OBie's New Year's Resolutions

On Mondays, I host a Facebook Book Club. Well, I don't really host it, my dog, OBie, does. It is for all ages, but the titles are absurd, yet real, book titles that 'actually' exist on Amazon. OBie and I discuss this ridiculousness with humor.

Since this past week's book title, which really wasn't at all bad this time, was entitled, Shante Keys and the New Year's Peas, it got OBie and me thinking about making resolutions in the new year. Do you make them and more importantly, do you keep them?

OBie had a few of his he shared at the book club meeting. He wanted you to know about them should you have a dog, or heaven forbid a cat (Just kidding! I miss my sidekick, Boo) and want to discuss with your pet about what kind of behaviors you want changed in the coming year. Here is OBie's list. See if you can relate to them if you own a dog.

1. I will try not to bark each time I hear a doorbell ring…on TV! (Or as my parents say when the bell goes off at the beginning of a round on Wheel of Fortune).
2. I will take my doggie pills without spitting them back out but only if they are wrapped in peanut butter or another yummy treat.
3. This one gets my goose: I am not going to feel bad should I pass gas around my immediate family. My dad does it and he doesn't feel bad. As a matter of fact, he laughs about it. And to think he is my role model.

4. I will try to become best friends and not bark too much like before at the mailman, mailwoman, or anyone else delivering packages or coming to knock at our front door. We have a glass front door, and it is so tempting to make sure they hear me. I am trying to protect my family after all, and they do leave soon after I start barking. And do I ever get thanked for that? No.

5. If I get sick in the middle of the night, I will try my best to make it to the tile area in the bathroom and not have an accident on my mama's expensive oriental rugs. I know she'll like this resolution.

6. I will be less afraid of the vacuum or other things that make loud noises. Right now, I am working on the street sweeper that cleans up our street once a week around five o'clock a.m. It has such a high pitch; it really bothers me. I can't promise getting over fireworks on the Fourth of July or New Year's Eve, though. My parents will still have to comfort me at those times for sure.

7. My mama and daddy are lucky I do not have to make a resolution about eating my poop or any other dog, cat, baby, or others' poop. To think I have some dog friends who do that! That's just gross. I am a gentleman.

8. But I still will not like my parents coming home from visiting another's home that owns a dog and smelling like their dog. It breaks my heart. Why couldn't I have gone with them? What were they doing without me? I love them so much, I might be a little jealous.

I'll keep you updated on my progress. Do you think I can keep these promises? Oh, and by the way...my mama and daddy are superstitious and enjoyed their collards, black eyes-peas, cornbread, pork, creamed corn, coleslaw, and carrot salad. I guess we really top off every new year with all these habits to cover our bases against any bad luck for the upcoming year.

Wind Beneath My Wings

"I am only living for you," she said the night before she died.

My parents married at thirty. I was their only child born ten years later. They called me a menopause baby as mother never had a chance at having another. And although I was a scamp and they were starting to tire because of the forty-year gap in our ages, they told me I brought joy into their world.

Before mother babied me, she babied my father for those ten years. When I came along, she babied us both. Once, many years later, Mother and I traveled to Hawaii and San Francisco as Daddy didn't have any interest in traveling like we wanted. In the 1970s we did not have a microwave yet. So, before we left on our trip, Mother cooked, labeled, and froze a meal for each night we would be away. For ten days! All my father had to do was take the meal out of the freezer and let it thaw before warming it up. "Nothing says loving like something from the oven."

And she pampered me my whole life, too. Criticized by her other mother friends who all had older offspring and "knew" best, she was told, "You are spoiling her." Mother always responded, "She's just well-loved."

Daddy died at seventy-one the year after I married. Mother lived another seventeen more. Growing up, it was a concern of mine that my parents wouldn't last as long as my friends' youthful parents. However, Mother made it to eighty-eight. I think that was pretty good. But I didn't marry young either and that put her at a double disadvantage. I was thirty-two when my first child was born.

In my mother's last years, I would take her to the doctor with second son in tow who was born when I was forty. There we were, like the Three Stooges – ages 84, 44, and 4. Our conversations went like this while Mother was holding on to her walker, "Mother, hurry up! Baby, slow down! Mother, hurry! Baby, wait up!" And I was sandwiched in the middle.

And she needed more attention than I could give. Because of my work, my husband, my two boys, I realized that my tender-loving-care wasn't enough as time went by. I needed help.

We chose a facility that took good care of her. I visited her three times a day. Sometimes I would set my alarm at 2:00 a.m. or many *different* morning times to pop in to see her so that the staff didn't count on my routine checks. I shouldn't have worried. They were angels themselves.

While Hubby was out of state during 2001's Veteran's Day weekend playing golf and watching the Auburn-Georgia football game, I visited mama and we watched the game on television. She and I both went to the University of Georgia to work towards our Master's in Education. My hubby went to Auburn.

After the game was over, not knowing it was her last night, I still loved kisses on my mother while saying goodnight. I told her to have a good night and I would see her in the morning. That's when she said it: *she was only living for me.*

I received the phone call of her passing around 6:30 a.m. as they had tried to reach me earlier, but I was in a sound sleep and Hubby was not around to hear the phone either.

I left quickly to get over to her room at the health facility. I spoke with the nurse on duty and asked if she could tell me anything about my mother's last moments. She said she had visited her room around 2:00 a.m. and when she returned at 3:00 a.m. she was gone.

I started making plans for her funeral. As an only child, my beautiful mother was everything to me: mother, neighbor, high school government teacher, friend, sister…she checked all the boxes. She was also a brainiac, where I was a social butterfly. She was diligent, I was all over the place. As that scamp, she still let me be me. Besides the traditional Presbyterian service, my cousin sang the Bette Midler title song, "Wind Beneath My Wings" from the movie, "Beaches."

I was heartbroken.

A year passed. It was again Veteran's Day weekend. Again, Hubby had that Monday off and was playing golf at another out-of-state destination. My mother died on Sunday, November 11, 2001. This Sunday, a year to the day of her passing, I was awakened by what I thought was a gentle noise coming from my husband's side of the bed. Drowsily, I started gaining my senses and realized it was his nightstand's radio playing music. I looked at the digital clock's time and it read 2:35 a.m. As I sat up and regained my senses, I heard the music coming from the radio and it was "Wind Beneath My Wings."

How could that be? How could it be exactly the year to the day of my mother's demise? How would she have known that song was sung at her funeral? She didn't request it, and I doubt she was even familiar with that movie or Bette Midler's songs? AND the third part to his equation was the

153

time of morning…between 2:00 a.m. and 3:00 a.m. It was a sign for sure. Mother was telling me what I had wondered many times…she died at 2:35 a.m. She was still around.

Crying, I then jumped out of bed and said aloud, "Hey, Mama! We are all okay. Now I know you are."

My faith grew that day. No sermon or religious pronouncements would ever give me that much comfort of an afterlife for us all. This was my special heavenly message as my mother let me know she was still with me as before: the 'wind beneath *my* wings'.

What Will Your Epitaph Say?

I have a favorite Presbyterian minister from all my years in church. I grew up in the Conyers Presbyterian Church but when I moved to Atlanta after college and before I married, I was a member of Peachtree Presbyterian Church on Roswell Road in Buckhead. It still is a megachurch and today averages about 3,200 in weekly worship. When I attended it was (and still is) one of the largest Presbyterian congregations in the United States of America. My pastor was Dr. Frank W. Harrington.

Perhaps you have heard of him? Dr. Harrington was the senior minister during the time when it was the largest Presbyterian (U.S.A.) church in North America. During his tenure, the church had fewer than 3,000 members when he arrived in 1971. When he died in 1999, there were more than 11,000.

He described Peachtree Presbyterian as "a big church that feels more like a small town" and he worked to keep that atmosphere. He cared about people and always knew his parishioners by name, understanding their circumstances, and tended to them in their time of need.

This man had a message! But he often peppered it with humor. I think that's why I felt so deeply about him. His humor helped me and I am sure others in his congregation to remember his messages. He performed my wedding ceremony in 1983. There was even a hic-cup in our ceremony that people talked about for a long time after (this comical blame goes to my hubby!).

I always asked the church office for a copy of each of his sermons because they inspired me when I needed his guidance again (still do) and one was entitled, WHAT WILL YOUR EPITAPH SAY? (February 11, 1990). We know that the word 'epitaph' is an inscription on or at a tomb or grave in memory of one buried there. The second definition, though, is more to the point: "a brief statement epitomizing a deceased person."

I truly think Dr. Harrington wouldn't mind if I took the liberty to have a little levity with this idea.

I have enjoyed my book with tombstone humor, *Famous Last Words & Tombstone Humor* by Gyles Brandreth. Some of the following epitaphs come from this book and some I researched on the internet. The ones I have found are mostly witty and I hope, as you read, you'll enjoy a bit of humor in these hesitant times we now find ourselves.

They may not all be true, but even so, I hope they provide a short chuckle to your day. Here are some engraved in stone.

J.R. Webb:
"Sticks and stones will break my bones
But words can never harm me."
Just my luck...they had plenty of sticks and stones.

No name:
Reincarnating: I'll be right back.
(So, don't touch my stuff!)

No name:
The shell is here
But the nut is gone.

Claire Voyance:
She should have seen it coming.

Herman Harband:
My wife Eleanor Arthur of Queens, N.Y.
Lived like a princess for 20 years traveling the
World with the best of everything.
When I went blind, she tried to poison me, took
All my money, all my medication, and left me alone
In the dark. Alone and sick, it's a miracle I escaped.
I won't see her in heaven because she's surely going to
hell.

Kay's Fudge (no last name):
2 sq. chocolate, 2 TBS. butter, melt on low heat.
Stir in 1 cup milk and bring to a boil.
Add 3 cups sugar, 1 TBS. vanilla, and pinch of salt.
Cook to soft ball stage. Pour on marble slab. Cool & beat*
& eat.
*(I don't make fudge so I don't know what it means to
beat on a marble slab before eating.)

Henry W. Neu, Jr.:
The black sheep of the family.
But I've had fun on this earth.

What would you like for your epitaph to say? Mine may
say, "In my defense, I was left unsupervised."

What Will Your Epitaph Say?
Part 2

I love to make people laugh and my speaking engagements create some of the best times when I can crack wise and there will be laughter afterwards.

I was asked to "perform" at the October 2020 Oak Hill Cemetery Tour in Newnan. Since the cemetery dates back to 1833 when Coweta County was still welcoming pioneer families, the graveyard carries some buried secrets of those who came before and since. The storytellers stood at several points throughout and told of a person or family who were either famous or infamous in Coweta County.

For my part, I was asked to dress up as a turn-of-the-century woman of means. My outfit was a custom-made floor length royal blue polyester silk dress buttoned in the back with large puff sleeves, high collar with a white lace jabot and a fake diamond brooch pin attached, white lace gloves, and a black velvet hat with veil, and another fake diamond pin added to it. I was supposed to be representative of some past grandeur of the town's families in "The City of Homes". (The gorgeous and grand homes of Newnan were spared because Sherman marched east to Savannah, as we well know.)

Oak Hill Cemetery is just as grand: elegant epitaphs, Victorian statuary, box tombs, and every style of marker from 1833. Among the engravings, I didn't find but one out of sync that only had the person's name and under it read, "She Died". No birth or death date.

There I was, as a gatekeeper, welcoming visitor groups as they entered the serene setting. Since I was asked to open wide the iron gates for guests to visit, and humorist that I am, I felt they should get their laughs on before entering the serious tone of their future stops. Here are some engraved inscriptions, not at Oak Hill, that I shared with the tour groups before entering.

These etchings are found in *Famous Last Words & Tombstone Humor* by Gyles Brandreth. Most are witty and I hope, as you read, you'll enjoy a bit of humor in them because in these hesitant times we now find ourselves, we still need a chuckle.

They may not all be verified, but even so, I hope they at least bring you a smile.

In memory of Mr. Peter Daniels
1688-1746
Beneath this stone, this lump of clay, lies uncle Peter Daniels,
Who too early in the month of May, took off his winter flannels.
Medway, Massachusetts

He called Bill Smith a liar.
Cripplecreek, Colorado

Sacred to the memory of Jared Bates
Who died Aug. the 6th ,1800
His widow, aged 24, lives at 7 Elm Street
Has every qualification for a good wife,
And yearns to be comforted.
Lincoln, Maine

In memory of Mrs. Alpha White, weight 309 lbs.
Open wide ye heavenly gates that lead to the heavenly
shore;
Our father suffered in passing through and mother
weighs much more.
Lee, Massachusetts

Here lies the body of John Mound
Lost at sea and never found.
Winslow, Maine

Shoot-'em-up-up-Jake
Ran for sheriff, 1872.
Ran for sheriff, 1876.
Buried, 1876.
Boot Hill Cemetery, Dodge City, Kansas

Played five aces,
Now playing the harp.
Boot Hill Cemetery, Dodge City, Kansas

Here lies the body of Susan Lowder
Who burst while drinking a Seidliz powder.
Called from this world to her Heavenly Rest
She should have waited till it effervesced. 1798
Burlington, New Jersey

And one of my all-time favorites:
Here lies Jane Smith, wife of Thomas Smith, marble
cutter.

This monument was erected by her husband as a tribute to
Her memory and specimen of his work.
Monuments of the same style 350 dollars.
Springdale, Ohio.

Made in the USA
Columbia, SC
31 December 2021